To Jordan
Lots of Love
Dad
17/8/08

SUBARU IMPREZA
TURBO

First published in April 2008

A catalogue record for this book is available from the British Library

ISBN 978 1 84425 497 2

Library of Congress control no. 2007943091

Published by Haynes Publishing,
Sparkford, Yeovil, Somerset BA22 7JJ, UK.
Tel: 01963 442030 Fax: 01963 440001
Int. tel: +44 1963 442030
Int. fax: +44 1963 440001
E-mail: sales@haynes.co.uk
Website: www.haynes.co.uk

Haynes North America Inc., 861 Lawrence Drive,
Newbury Park, California 91320, USA

Design and layout by Richard Parsons

Printed and bound in Britain by J. H. Haynes & Co. Ltd,
Sparkford, Yeovil, Somerset BA22 7JJ

AUTOCAR
COLLECTION
SUBARU IMPREZA
TURBO

Haynes Publishing

CONTENTS

Autocar Collection: Subaru Impreza

The best words, photos and data from the world's oldest car magazine

INTRODUCTION

Chas Hallett
Editor, *Autocar*

The most remarkable thing about Subaru is how steadfastly the company has always stuck to the same set of non-conformist design principles through multiple generations of models. It has been designing its cars with nose-mounted, turbocharged flat-four engines and full-time four-wheel-drive, a mechanical recipe unique to the sector, for close to four decades.

Subaru's idiosyncratic engineers have polished and perfected the natural advantages of their system (compactness, low centre of gravity, class-leading traction and stability) and matched it with a ruggedness of construction that has gradually bred a whole family tree of winning rally cars, which can nowadays be found in every serious rally competition across the world.

Unlike other companies that have discovered motor sport and embraced exotic formulae in a headlong desire to win, Subaru has only ever used the cars it makes for the mass market in competition – or at least their essential structures and mechanical parts – with the result that the increasingly high performance and fine handling of its competition cars has been able to influence and improve the sportier production offerings.

Subaru's astute move during the mid-'90s to start offering production facsimiles of its championship-winning rally cars has not only established names like WRX and STi in the highest echelons of motoring lore, but bred a whole genre of affordable yet super-fast saloons on a plane above mere hot hatchbacks. It also did much to assemble a whole generation of drivers that especially loved the WRX/EVO/RS brand of performance – and still do.

Which is where this 14-year collection of 29 of *Autocar*'s fast Subaru features comes in. As the world's oldest motoring magazine, we've tested them all, but these are the edited highlights. Together, they describe and explain the high-performance Subaru phenomenon, through the eyes of the world's most experienced testers and photographers. We believe they add up to a unique insight, which we hope you will enjoy.

IMPREZA 2000 TURBO

There's no doubting the rally car in its blood, not least because it can leave a Cossie or Integrale standing

It all starts as a staccato, burping hiccup of a roar, distant and mysterious through the forest gloom. Your pulse rate will rise quite involuntarily. Seconds later a screaming, spitting white metal monster will hurl itself, usually sideways and quite often airborne, through the shivering firs. This is rallying, one of motorsport's most visceral events, and for decades now one of the best ways for manufacturers to invest mundane motors with unspeakable glory. Lancia's Delta would be a forgotten name if not for the legendary Integrale, and who'd have thought a plain old Escort could be as painfully desirable as the RS Cosworth?

And while Subaru's Impreza offers up a pretty yawn-making road presence, the full-house rally version is about as dull as a taxi ride through Beirut.

Now, for a non-princely £17,499, Subaru will deliver an Impreza Turbo 2000 4wd that strikes a rallying pose while threatening Integrale-busting performance.

A split second after turning the key you'll know this Impreza isn't bluffing; the free-revving engine possesses a bassy, coarse voice that says you'd better believe the 208bhp, 201lb ft power and torque figures in the brochure. However, those figures are produced at 6000 and 4800rpm respectively, demanding that the horizontally opposed four sings hard for its supper.

QUICK FACTS

Model	Subaru Impreza 2000 Turbo
Price as tested	£17,718
Top speed	137mph
0–60mph	5.8sec
MPG	18.7
For	Fabulous performance, good value for money, excellent warranty
Against	Dull grey cabin, baulky gearchange, thirsty engine

ROAD TEST

6 APRIL 1994

Volume 200

No 1 | 5070

Britain's best car magazine

AUTOCAR & Motor

208bhp
0-60 in
5.8sec
£17,499
Subaru Impreza Turbo

First Full Road Test of 1994's Most Important New Family Saloon
RENAULT LAGUNA

ABOVE Impreza announces serious intent with dinner-plate-sized foglights and more scoops and vents than an F16.

RIGHT Massively secure handling aided by four-wheel drive and grippy Michelins. Very quick point-to-point.

OPPOSITE Engine is a mildly tweaked version of Legacy Turbo powerplant. It delivers stunning performance but isn't the most refined.

The Impreza's turbocharged and intercooled powerplant is effectively a mildly tweaked version of the four-cam 197bhp engine that serves in the Legacy Turbo, itself no slouch.

You won't find much power spilling uselessly on to the pavement, either, with a viscous-coupled four-wheel-drive chassis that senses when a wheel is about to let go and sends the horses elsewhere. In normal, dry-road motoring, the torque split is about equal, front to rear. A relatively short-geared five-speed manual gearbox delivers the urge to grippy 205/55 tyres that ride on 15in rims. And the whole package weighs just 1213kg, giving the Impreza a better power-to-weight ratio than even the mighty Integrale.

Launch this unlikely junior supercar off the line in absolutely ideal conditions – a soaking wet track on a cool morning – and a scarcely believable 5.8sec later you will be travelling at 60mph. Even though the Impreza will do it all without leaving second gear, that is still a damned impressive result, one that tops the Escort Cosworth, Integrale and, just to shut the snide boys up, a Porsche 968 as well.

As we have already intimated, though, the 0–60mph figure is by no means a definitive performance yardstick, and while the Impreza will stay with the Escort Cosworth and Integrale up to about 75mph, from that point forward the other two will pull out in front. Given a little time to catch up, the keen-hearted Impreza will match the best with its 137mph top speed. And in the 30–70mph sprint the Impreza impresses with its 6.6sec figure, as good as the Integrale or Cosworth.

The Impreza behaves a little like its big brother, the Legacy, with turbo lag evident at low revs and less electric throttle response than its high-torque competitors. From about 3500 up to its 7000rpm red line the Impreza delivers a smoothly consistent rush of turbo thrust. It is an addictive sensation and one that will soon have you forgiving the engine for its somewhat coarse, unrefined manners.

You may find it less easy to forgive the gearbox, which is slow and rubbery at best and can baulk badly if you try to hurry it along.

The Impreza Turbo isn't just a straight-line thrill merchant. Responsibly doling out portions of its 208bhp to the most deserving wheels, it provides safe handling through fast, tight corners. That sense of security is helped out by the excellent grip offered up by the Michelin Pilots. Steam into a corner too quickly and the Impreza will start to run wide, with gentle and predictable understeer sending an early warning of relinquishing grip. Raising your right foot a shade tightens the line accurately and effortlessly, though. Simply put the Impreza feels confidently neutral, benign even, in most situations. With uprated springs and dampers, it corners flat too, but string a series of fast bends together and the Impreza can begin to feel unsettled, as if it needs a little more time to recover from the last corner. And the steering, while precise, is touch too light for a car of the Impreza's meaty aspirations.

Ultimately, the Impreza is an easy car to drive quickly on challenging roads, but really keen drivers might resent the lack of involvement in the process; this Subaru is quite content to let its competent four-wheel-drive chassis take all of the credit for a tight, well-executed corner.

The suspension's added stiffness does no favours for the ride, though. Over country roads with quick undulations and the usual blemishes the Impreza pogos about in a nervous and unsettling manner. The picture

ROAD TEST IMPREZA TURBO

ACCELERATION FROM REST

True mph	seconds	speedo mph
30	1.7	33
40	3.0	43
50	4.4	54
60	5.8	65
70	8.3	77
80	11.1	88
90	13.7	98
100	18.7	108
110	24.8	120

Standing qtr mile 14.7sec/92mph
Standing km 27.5sec/114mph
30–70mph through gears 6.6sec

ACCELERATION IN GEAR

MPH	5th	4th	3rd	2nd
10–30	-	-	6.7	4.1
20–40	16.2	9.9	5.4	3.0
30–50	15.3	8.8	4.2	2.4
40–60	15.1	6.8	3.6	2.7
50–70	13.4	5.9	3.9	-
60–80	11.6	6.7	4.3	-
70–90	10.2	7.5	-	-
80–100	11.8	-	-	-
90–110	-	-	-	-

MAXIMUM SPEEDS

5th 137mph/6,000rpm	4th 120/7,000
3rd 85/7,000	2nd 60/7,000
1st 34/7,000	

BRAKES

30/50/70mph	11.3/31.6/62.8m
St qtr mile	104.0m @ 92mph

FUEL CONSUMPTION

Overall mpg on test		18.7mpg
Best/worst on test		26.7/9.5
Touring*		26.7mpg
Range		356 miles
Tank capacity		60 litres
Govt tests	Urban	24.8mpg
	56mph	39.8mpg
	75mph	30.1mpg

WEIGHT

Kerb (incl half tank)	1,213kg
Distribution f/r	54/46%
Max payload	550kg
Max towing weight	500kg

* Achieved over a pre-set test route designed to replicate an average range of driving conditions. The figures were taken at Millbrook proving ground, with the odometer reading 3500 miles. Autocar & Motor test results are protected by world copyright and may not be reproduced without the editor's written permission

WHAT IT COSTS

IMPREZA 2000 TURBO

List price	£17,499
Total as tested	£17,718

INSURANCE

Insurance	Group 17

WARRANTY

Three years/60,000 miles, six years corrosion, three years roadside recovery

SERVICING

Major 15,000 miles, 4.25hr, parts £42.50

Interim 7,500 miles, 2.2hr, parts £42.50

PARTS COSTS

Set spark plugs	£60.00
Brake pads front	£88.12
Brake pads rear	£85.00
Exhaust (exc cat)	£802.52
Door mirror glass	£90.47
Tyre (each, typical)	£153.15
Windscreen	£203.96

EQUIPMENT CHECKLIST

Electric sunroof	£799
Driver's airbag	■
Metallic paint	**£219**
Adjustable seatbelt height	■
Variable speed intermittent wipe	■
Electrically adjustable mirrors	■
Auto-reverse radio/cassette player	■
Number of speakers	4
Remote hatch/boot release	■
Split/folding rear seat	■
Power steering	■
Alloy wheels	■
Adjustable steering column	■
Electric windows all round	■
Central locking	■
Height and tilt adj driver's seat	■
Anti-lock brakes	■
Anti-theft system	■
Front foglights	■

Options in **bold** fitted to test car

■ = Standard na = not available

Impreza Turbo doesn't skimp on the goodies; central locking, electric windows and driver's airbag are all standard fit.

is a bit brighter on the motorway, where occasional disturbances are dealt with swiftly without any reverberations through the bodyshell.

Drive the Impreza the way its spoilered, scooped and vented bonnet suggests and the fuel pump penalty is severe. We managed a touring economy of just 26.7mpg and overall consumption of 18.7mpg, which is, frankly, poor when cars like the Cosworth will manage at least 20mpg overall.

The initial bright promise of the Impreza's astonishing performance is further let down once the light, pillar-less doors are slammed shut, ensconcing occupants in an unrelentingly grey cocoon of nastily textured cloth and indifferent quality plastics. The height-adjustable driver's seat is supportive in most situations, and a fine driving position is helped out by an adjustable steering column, but this cabin's monochrome blandness is completely at odds with the car's shocking pink performance.

Also, those pillar-less doors contribute to an irritating amount of wind noise at motorway speeds.

However unpleasantly executed the Impreza's cabin is, it does have plenty of Sainsbury's sensibility. The boot is an average size for the class, but folding

DIMENSIONS

Interior width front/rear 1,410/1,410mm **Min/max boot width** 980/1,360mm
VDA boot volume seats up/down 0.35/0.60cu m **Front/rear tracks** 1460/1450mm
Kerb weight 1,213kg **Weight dist. front/rear** 54/46% **Width** 1,690mm inc mirrors

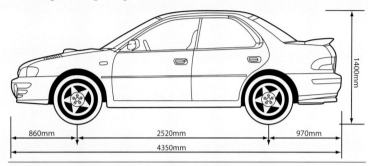

1400mm

860mm   2520mm   970mm
4350mm

ENGINE

Layout	4 cyl, horizontally opposed, 1,994cc
Max power	208bhp/6,000rpm
Max torque	201lb ft/4,800rpm
Specific output	104bhp per litre
Power to weight	171bhp per tonne
Installation	longitudinal, front, four-wheel drive
Construction	Aluminium head and block
Bore/stroke	92/75mm
Valve gear	4 per cyl, dohc
Compression	8.0:1
Ignition and fuel	Electronic ignition, multi-point fuel injection

CHASSIS AND BODY

Body	Cd 0.37
Wheels	5x16in Alloy
Tyres	205/55 R15 Michelin Pilot HX
Spare	Space saver

TRANSMISSION

Gearbox 5-speed manual
Ratios/mph per 1,000rpm
Final drive 4.11

1st	3.45/4.8	2nd	1.95/8.6
3rd	1.37/12.2	4th	0.97/17.2
5th	0.74/22.5		

SUSPENSION

Front Struts, coils, transverse link
Rear Struts, coils, transverse link, trailing arms

STEERING

Type Power-assisted rack and pinion
Turns lock-to-lock 2.8
Turning circle 10.4m

BRAKES

Front 228mm disc
Rear 230mm disc
Anti-lock Standard

rear seats almost double its load capacity. Front headroom is generous, especially when the pricey £799 sunroof option is left off the check list. Rear legroom is surprisingly good, too, but a low rear roof lining spoils headroom for even the modestly tall.

At £17,499 for the saloon and £17,999 for the oddly aspected estate, the Impreza Turbo offers more practical performance than anything else for the money (an Escort Cosworth costs £22,500 and a Delta Integrale £25,000). On that score alone, the Impreza is great value for money, but Subaru adds a generous specification to the mix; a driver's airbag, electric windows, alloy wheels and central locking are all standard. The only sour note, and it is a fairly rude one, is the knowledge that the Impreza Turbo is likely to cost a small fortune to insure.

Even though the Impreza fails to convince as a stand alone champion in the mould of a Cosworth or Integrale, Subaru's little rocket is still a stunning accomplishment. An enthusiast with less than £18,000 could never hope to find himself behind the wheel of a sophisticated four-wheel-drive chassis backed by Cosworth levels of performance. Not until the Impreza Turbo 2000, that is.

FOREST FLIER

IMPREZA TURBO Subaru's rally-bred Impreza is quicker yet £5000 cheaper than an Escort Cossie. So what's the catch? Peter McSean reports after 12,000 miles

I could see in the rear view mirror that the besuited bloke standing behind the Subaru wasn't about to move. Odd behaviour in a multi-storey car park, so I climbed out to see why. "Sorry," he said hesitantly, "but I just had to ask: is it true what they say about your car in the road tests? I'm thinking of getting one instead of a BMW 318i S, after Colin McRae won the RAC Rally... I was there, you know..."

Here was walking confirmation of precisely why we had chosen to put a four-wheel-drive, turbocharged Impreza on our fleet. Precisely, but not exclusively. Colin & Carlos Inc were going to give the car street cred by giving it streaked crud and that was an important factor in our choice, certainly, but there was an even better reason for running the hot Subaru. Over to you, *Road Test Yearbook*: "[The Impreza Turbo 2000 4wd is the] bargain of the year... quite possibly the performance buy of the decade."

Sure, it was cheap to buy at £17,499 when Escort Cossies were listed at £22,535, but would it also be cheap to run? Or would there be a hidden appetite for oil, tyres, hoses, turbos, brake pads or driveshafts? Would the areas where Subaru has cut costs prove too much of a compromise day in, day out? Could anyone live with such a dull interior, for instance? Would the car be a target for thieves? And would the tin box shake itself to pieces after four months? Surely you only get what you pay for, and a car that covers 0–60mph in 5.5sec on its way to 137mph doesn't come that cheap unless there's a catch. Somewhere.

Well, if there is a catch we've yet to find it, 12,000 miles on. So far we've enjoyed the legendary Subaru reliability which gives the company so much repeat business. So far that bland cabin has mattered only to those who drive the car occasionally; frequent drivers soon don't notice it or find compensations elsewhere.

You don't have to look far. For a start there's the two-litre blown flat four, the performance of which

OUR CARS

15 MARCH 1995

Volume 203

No 11 | 5118

AUTOCAR

Watch out MG!

Renault's new sports car is here

Plus Ford's New Mini

This Week: MG Wows Geneva Bargain XJ6s
Mansell's Crisis Celica Cabrio Portugal Rally

improved markedly between 4000 and 8000 miles. Wielding 208bhp at 6000rpm and 201lb ft at 4800rpm, the 1213kg Subaru puts its power and torque down remarkably efficiently. Take its McLaren F1-equalling 0–30mph time of 1.8sec, or its 0–100 in 16.0, 30–70mph in 5.7, standing quarter mile in 14.3 (95mph). Then there's 50–70mph in fifth in 10.5sec, 30–50mph in fourth in 7.9sec. And for overtaking on country lanes, how about 50–70mph in third in 3.4sec? Or 30–50mph in second in 2.3sec?

Normally such acceleration is the preserve of supercars. Seldom is it offered by a car as versatile as an Impreza. In six months, our Subaru with the long name has been involved in two house moves (a fine workhorse with worthwhile space inside the car, provided you can access it through the narrow boot opening); transported five adults (one too many after about 30 minutes); acted as chase car on the RAC (a superb all-rounder); been the organiser's car for the London–Edinburgh Trial (reliability and speed proven again, this time in blizzard conditions); done more 200-mile midnight runs than I care to remember (where its easy cruising, lack of foibles and good seats and driving position mattered more than its choppy A-road/ motorway ride); and trundled around and lived on London streets most days (where its Cobra three-circuit immobiliser has helped to keep it where we parked it). We've also admired its impeccable manners, gearing that lets it trickle along in traffic without feathering the clutch, its ability to pull out into small gaps without bogging down, good all-round visibility and 4340mm by 1690mm town-friendly dimensions.

Through it all, our super Sub has maintained a virtually faultless reliability record, needing no attention outside its scheduled services at 1000 miles (£34.78) and 7500 miles (£148.26). If those sums seem large, bear two things in mind: the

'THERE ARE FEW OTHER CARS CAPABLE OF STAYING WITH THE RALLY-BRED SUBARU, AND NONE AT THIS PRICE'

M54 KJW had first taste of UK at Jarrow Slake, Tyne dock. 18 days later we drove it away from Holbeins.

only other outlay has been for petrol (a gallon every 24.2 miles on average), and the labour rate at our nearest Subaru dealer, Holbeins in London SW8, was a hefty £44.50 per hour. Though fairly typical for a London Subaru dealer, a quick ring round showed the £30 mark to be common for most parts of the country, with mid £30s in more densely populated areas. For top money you'd expect Holbein to be efficient, polite and collect/deliver the car during servicing, and that was the case.

So what's with the virtually faultless? Well, from delivery we felt the volume of air coming in through the ventilation system was inadequate. At the 7500-mile service Holbein gave it a thorough examination but could find no fault. However, the throughput of air seems to have increased, so we can only conclude that Holbein cured it inadvertently. Even so, the rear side windows and back screen still mist up easily in the wet and those who've forked out £1,499 for the optional air conditioning say it's been worth every penny.

It's one of the small compromises I'm prepared to accept – though I don't think I should have to – in exchange for low-cost, high-thrill driving.

There are others, such as the absence of low fuel and screen wash warning lights, the difficulty during daylight of seeing if the air recirculation button is lit or not, the lack of a light in the glovebox, central locking that works only from the driver's door and lacks a remote, bootlid hinges that intrude into the luggage area, the absence of a rheostat to alter the brightness of the instruments, and a reduction

ABOVE This was it until odo read 1,000 miles; spacious boot once past narrow opening; purposeful front view hints at supercar performance.

WHAT COLIN'S CROWD CAN DO FOR YOU

There is nothing wrong with how a standard Impreza Turbo handles. It's a tad soft at the front and understeers a bit in the wet if you're being picky, but that's about it. However, the folk behind Colin McRae's car, Prodrive (tel: 01295 273355), open up new levels of handling for road-going Impreza Turbo drivers. And they do so with Subaru's blessing. Stiffer, tuned suspension (£1,322) means negligible body roll and minimal understeer, replacing the standard car's front-drive feel with greater stability, balance and poise. The stiffer front end also reduces weight transference under braking, avoiding the regular car's predilection for activating the anti-lock earlier than anticipated. The ride is hard, not helped by £1,645 205/45 ZR17s, but we think keen drivers will accept the trade-off. Other wheel/tyre choices are on offer, as is a well-executed interior retrim at £1,972. Our advice? Go the whole hog if you have the funds (£4929 all in). If not, start saving for the suspension mods.

ABOVE The Sub stood the heat during Adam Harper's Sinclair C5 tunnel of fire stunt.

RIGHT Tight fit but basics easy to access; Impreza makes remarkably efficient use of its copious power and torque.

in front passenger legroom due to an ECU behind the bulkhead.

And while I'm glad that the radio/cassette is removable by me rather than a thief, there have been plenty of occasions when I've found it inconvenient carting the whole unit around.

Yet I've appreciated the little things it gets right, such as being able to reach the manual aerial without moving my back off the driver's seat and the backlighting that makes the digital clock readable in sunlight. Then there's the way the headlights switch off when the ignition is off (parking lights are on a separate circuit), and the fact that there's a cradle on the fuel filler flap to hold the cap while you pour in the preferred choice of super unleaded (the higher octane level does make a difference to performance).

And we mustn't overlook the ease of entry and exit from any of the Impreza's seats, the logical placement of the controls in the cabin, one-shot driver's window, good-sized door pockets and glovebox, headlamp washers, well-shaped seats, driver's airbag (never used), superb main beam illumination (pity the dipped beams are such a disappointment), easily folded rear seats and a

0.60cu m capacity once done, 10.4-metre turning circle, three-year/60,000-mile warranty including Europe-wide breakdown recovery... the list goes on.

Above all, though, our Impreza impresses most for its point-to-point prowess, in all weathers. For the full story read our road test (pages 8–13), but for a compressed taster, read on. The one bar of boost means that you dictate your own velocity along twisting roads instead of finding your speed restricted by some bozzo towing a caravan or the two cars stuck behind it. While capable of improvement (see panel on p17), the standard car's safe handling still entertains. Throw in strong brakes and an unerring ability to put the power down out of a corner long before most other cars could dare and there are few other cars capable of staying with the rally-bred Subaru, and none at this price.

Yet more astonishing still is how easy and economical it is to live with on a daily basis. Bargain of the year? After 12,000 miles, all the evidence indicates that our *Road Test Yearbook* conclusion is spot on – both for buying the car and for running it. Would we recommend this rocket for small pockets? Wholeheartedly. Believe it, Mr Suit in the car park, or it's your loss.

LOGBOOK IMPREZA TURBO

TEST STARTED 18.08.94
Mileage at start	208
Mileage now	12,177
Colour	Flame red
Options floor mats	£44

WHAT IT COST
Price new then, basic/with options
£17,499/£17,543
Price new now, basic/with options
£17,999/£17,543
Estimated resale value to dealer
£12,500
Depreciation
£5,000/28.5 per cent

TYRES
205/55 ZR15 Michelin Pilot HX
Percentage worn front/rear at 12,177miles
40/40 per cent (tyres swapped front to rear at 6,985 miles)
Typical cost each £200

FUEL/OIL
Average fuel consumption	24.2mpg
Best/worst mpg	27.3/17.5
Oil (non service)	0

INSURANCE
Example 1 35-year-old married male with clean licence, five years' no-claims bonus, car garaged in low-risk Oxfordshire **£601**
Example 2 25-year-old single male with two speeding convictions, five years' no-claims and car not garaged in reasonably high-risk Middlesex **£1,366**
Source: Quotel

ENGINE
Layout 4 cylinders horizontally opposed, 1,994cc
Max power 208bhp at 6,000rpm
Max torque 201lbft at 4,800rpm
Top speed 137mph*
0–60mph 5.5sec*
30–70mph through gears 5.7sec*
*Recorded at Millbrook Proving Ground with odometer reading 8,107. Surface dry

DIMENSIONS
Length	4,340mm
Width	1,690mm
Height	1,400mm
Wheelbase	2,520mm
Kerb weight	1,213kg

SERVICING
1,137 miles	£34.78
6,985 miles	£148.26

REPAIRS AND FAULTS
None (but see text about the ventilation system)

SOLD BY
Subaru (UK) Ltd, Ryder Street, West Bromwich, West Midlands, B70 0EJ. Tel: 0121 522 2000

FOR
Point-to-point ability, easy-going in town, cheap, McRae drives one

AGAINST
Narrow boot opening, unsettled ride, mists up in the wet

ROAD-GOING RALLY CARS

IMPREZA WRX Who do you think you are, Colin McRae, Tommi Mäkinen, Carlos Sainz? Andrew Golby drives the road-going versions of the world's greatest rally cars

Winter in a job like this can be a miserable experience. Days start and end in the dark, photographers grumble about poor light and journalists get tired of washing the same car half a dozen times a day. It seems that as soon as a wheel turns, it's just as filthy as it started.

But every now and then a little bit of bad weather can be a good thing. And this is one such occasion.

We have gathered the three finest rally car-inspired road machines available. Just yesterday (Tuesday) you could have seen the full-house versions thundering across the Welsh countryside in the Network Q RAC Rally. But you don't need to be Colin McRae to get a taste of these cars.

We have the ultimate Subaru Impreza, with a name so long that it barely fits on the bootlid. The WRX Type R STi, Version III is a bit of a mouthful in English, so we'll save you the Japanese translation.

We already know that the Mitsubishi Lancer Evo IV is a useful tool; back in April we drove this very car and came away deeply impressed. Neither of these two cars is available from your local dealership, but both are on sale through personal import specialists.

And then there's the Escort. It's a bit of a ringer in this company, we'll admit. It's not quite what it appears to be, but it isn't far off. Ford has built it to give a taste of what the real World Rally Car is like. It's stripped, caged, tuned and comes complete with an intercom and, crucially, an anti-lag kit.

This is the device which makes rally cars sound as if somebody has stuffed a box of fireworks up the exhaust pipe. It also just happens to keep the boost at a constant pressure, thereby eliminating nearly all turbo lag. Our only justification for it being here is to have some fun. You could buy one, but it would cost the best part of £250,000, and it isn't quite as versatile as the £30,000 Impreza or £28,000 Lancer.

Still, we're going to enjoy finding out that it isn't best suited to the school run.

Our venue is Warwickshire, my home county.

FEATURE

26 NOVEMBER 1997

Volume 214

No 8 | 5257

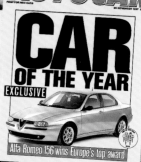

AUTOCAR

CAR
OF THE YEAR

EXCLUSIVE

Alfa Romeo 156 wins Europe's top award

ON TEST
New VW
Golf GTi

SECRET
Vauxhall's
hot Vectra

PACKED WITH
QUALITY USED
CARS FOR SALE

ABOVE Frenetic
Subaru's super-close
'box and great-sounding
flat four engine spur
it from 0–60mph in
blistering 4.9sec.

OPPOSITE TOP
Fearsome Escort is
explosively quick, but the
faster you go, harder it is
to drive; Lancer lightning
quick across country, but
quite civilised, too, with
comfortable ride.

The place is littered with enjoyable and often quiet B-roads – perfect fodder for cars such as these.

It's a crazy express train that people see: first a bright yellow streak flashes past, followed by a silver projectile with a huge rear wing and, to top it all off, a full-bore rally car comes popping and banging past. Tom Salt, who's taking the pictures, has a harder job than normal on his hands. Before he can start work, he has to persuade the rest of us to stop driving for a minute; and we're not keen.

I'd started the day in the Escort, driving halfway round the M25 and then up the M1. It isn't much fun on roads like that. After about 60 miles the intercom is brought into play. The ear defender headphones quieten everything down and work so well that I can hear my passenger's every breath. We put up with a bone-jarring ride, confident that the Ford will come good later.

Meanwhile, the other two are happily cruising along. Both have an astonishingly-supple ride quality considering their roots, especially the Lancer. Noise refinement is pretty good, too, although the Impreza is a little louder, because of its shorter gearing.

By mid-morning we leave the motorway and don't rejoin until darkness falls; it's our best move of the day. The roads are pretty wet at the moment, but signs of slightly better weather are in the sky. Still in the Escort, our hardcore player here, I realise it was just as well that I never harboured any ideas about forging a career in a rally car. It's a fearsome machine, definitely the fastest car of the three, demanding the most respect from its driver. Only the instrument binnacle reminds you that this is an Escort, and even that has a competition car row of red lights, which illuminate when the red line is fast approaching.

On start-up, a noisy fuel pump whirs from the boot area, you belt up the five-point harness, and wonder how not to hit anything while reversing. The huge rear wing renders the back window almost academic and half-size wing mirrors don't help, either.

'THE IMPREZA IS ONE OF THOSE CARS THAT CANNOT BE DRIVEN IN ANY MANNER OTHER THAN TOO FAST'

PASSENGER POWER

Scarce on comfort, big on technology – that's the Escort. It's got just as much power as the pukka WRC contender (300bhp), but is a bit short on torque. An incredible 442lb ft is on offer to Carlos Sainz and Juha Kankkunen; this car has 'just' 258lb ft. It's also equipped with, of all things, a Sierra 4x4's gearbox. The real deal has a six-speed sequential unit. The best fun can be had by the co-driver with the Pectel control system. Everything from revs, boost, temperature and even throttle angle can be determined by the on-car computer. The passenger also has a horn control on the footplate.

Still, none of this matters once you're on the right road, and as someone at Ford points out, "Carlos Sainz doesn't need to know where he's been, he's only worried about where he's going." Fair point.

You go very fast everywhere in the Escort, and although it outpaces both the Lancer and the Impreza with ease, it's more intimidating than both of them. With the anti-lag switched off (exhaust life is dramatically reduced when it's on) there's a noticeable delay, but once it kicks in, the power is explosive. And a satisfyingly dramatic whistle from the turbo leaves no doubt that this car is serious.

Drive the Ford at a controlled pace and it's quite good fun, but when you try to up the speeds the car becomes more difficult. Body roll is minimal and there's simply massive grip and traction from its 235/40 Michelin Pilots. Judging the limit with the accurate but light steering is also quite difficult.

Braking power is something else. Huge 15in, eight-pot caliper items are fitted up front, backed up by 12in four-pot stoppers at the rear. But there is so much noise and paraphernalia surrounding you that it's a little hard to relax and let it all flow.

This is never a problem in either Japanese machine, especially the Impreza. The Subaru scorches through

All three cars show true mettle on greasy roads such as this.

BRACE YOURSELF FOR 10MPG

It's attention to detail that makes the WRX special. The best example is the carbon fibre brace that stretches across the engine bay. Quite apart from looking magnificent, it increases the rigidity of the two-door Impreza bodyshell. To find an extra 72bhp (over the standard Impreza turbo) there's a different ECU, forged steel pistons, lightweight hollow valves, a bigger radiator and that intercooler with a manually or automatically operated water spray. A toughened rear axle, clutch cover and transmission complete the specification. Just don't expect decent fuel economy: go really hard and you won't crack 10mpg.

RIGHT Escort facia recognisable from standard car; highlight of Lancer's cabin is Momo wheel, which looks as good as it feels.

BELOW Subaru, Mitsubishi have identical power, torque: 300bhp, 260lb ft; Escort's 258lb ft down from 442lb ft.

each of its five gears at a blistering rate. It's one of those cars that can't be driven in any manner other than too fast. You're constantly shocking yourself and any passengers with the speed at which you're travelling. A reassuring chassis offers all the encouragement needed to hurtle into corners at huge speeds.

This is also possible in the Lancer, although its handling bias seems to favour a shade more understeer on turn-in. Both cars have monster levels of traction, and on greasy roads even second gear corners provoke only a nudge of natural power oversteer on the exit of a bend.

The flat four Subaru engine produces 280bhp at 6500rpm in this trim, and a gutsy 260lb ft of torque at 4000rpm. Between gearchanges there's a momentary pause before the power (and the turbocharger) comes on again, hurling you further and faster up the road. The ratios are super-close, designed to work within the limited top speed of 112mph. As a result, it takes only 4.9sec to reach 60mph. Despite its extra power, the distinctive flat four growl isn't any more urgent than the standard car's. That said, it's still a great noise.

From a driver's point of view, the Lancer isn't quite so aurally inspiring. The Evolution IV sounds better from the outside, coming into earshot well before your eyes catch sight of it. And it has the best gearchange of all three cars here, being slicker and faster than either the slightly imprecise Ford 'box or the accurate but notchy Impreza shift. Overall, it feels marginally slower than the Impreza, but on the road there's really nothing in it. In the 280bhp Mitsubishi's favour, it's slightly less frenetic and a little more refined

than the more focused Impreza. Over a year of driving, we think that difference could really count.

It doesn't steer with quite the same authority as the Subaru, either, but we're talking small differences here. The WRX has wonderfully fluid and uncorrupted feedback, thanks in part to a rear-wheel-drive bias. In comparison, the Evo IV's helm is slightly lighter and loses a little in its feel. It does, however, sport the best wheel, with a delightful-looking and feeling Momo item. It's the highlight of the Lancer's cabin.

The Impreza's interior is pretty mundane. The Japanese love their gadgets, though, and both the Subaru and Mitsubishi have dashboard-operated water sprays for the intercooler. In the Impreza there's also a rocker switch to divert power between the front and rear wheels. As much as 50 per cent of torque can be diverted to the front.

All three cars have first rate driving positions, although the Impreza's good looking seats lack lower back support on long journeys.

ABOVE Subaru's gadgets include dashboard-operated water spray for intercooler.

'THE LANCER'S LESS FRENETIC THAN THE IMPREZA. OVER A YEAR THAT DIFFERENCE COULD REALLY COUNT'

ABOVE Escort's £250k price tag dwarfs £30k, £28k needed for Impreza, Lancer.

RIGHT Reassuring Subaru encourages you to throw it into corners at huge speeds.

Putting the Ford aside as a frivolous toy – one to order when your lottery numbers come up – choosing between the other two is a difficult task. Both are so well suited to UK roads and driving conditions that it seems ludicrous they can only be bought through the back door. The Lancer's subtle "edge design" look is more appealing than the Subaru's neat but plain two-door shape, but the Impreza is slightly more fun to drive.

If I had to choose, I'd take the Impreza, but to be honest I really need both. Summer could never end quickly enough – just bring me those greasy, dirty, dark roads.

EVOLUTION IMPROVES THE BREED

The Lancer is a seriously well honed piece of engineering. This is the fourth evolution special that Mitsubishi has built to Group A rallying regulations. This means that 2,500 have to be built to allow it to take part in the world championship. It was through Group A that we got cars such as the Lancia Delta Integrale and through the preceding class (Group B) that Audi Sport Quattros and Ford RS200s were built. The Escort and Impreza compete in the new World Rally Car class, which doesn't require any road cars to be built at all.

FACTFILE

MAKE	FORD	MITSUBISHI	SUBARU
Model	**ESCORT WRC**	**LANCER EVO IV**	**IMPREZA WRX**
On-the-road price	£250,000 (est)	£28,000 (est)	£30,000
Cost per mile	-	-	-
Insurance group	20	20	20
0–60mph	4.9sec	n/a	4.9sec
Top speed	137mph	n/a	112mph (limited)
Length	4,211mm	4,330mm	4,340mm
Width	1,738mm	1,690mm	1,690mm
Height	1,400mm	1,400mm	1,405mm
Wheelbase	2,552mm	2,510mm	2,520mm
Weight	1230kg	n/a	1,240kg
Engine layout	4 cyls in line, 1,993cc	4 cyls in line, 1,997cc	4 cyls, horiz opposed, 1,994cc
Max power	300bhp/6,000rpm	280bhp/6,500rpm	280bhp/6,500rpm
Max torque	258lb ft/3,200rpm	260lb ft/3,000rpm	260lb ft/4,000rpm
Specific output	151bhp/litre	140bhp/litre	140bhp/litre
Power to weight	244bhp/tonne	n/a	226bhp/tonne
Installation	Transverse, front, four-wheel drive	Transverse, front, four-wheel drive	Longitudinal, front, four-wheel drive
Made of	Alloy head, iron block	Alloy head, iron block	Alloy head and block
Bore/stroke	90.8/77mm	85/88mm	92/75mm
Valve gear	4 per cyl, dohc	4 per cyl, dohc	4 per cyl, dohc
Ignition and fuel	Ford S8 electronic ignition, Garrett T4 turbocharger	ECI-Multi point, Mitsubishi electronics, Mitsubishi Heavy Industries TDOSH turbocharger	Electronic ignition, multi-point injection, turbocharger
Front suspension	MacPherson struts, coils, dampers, anti-roll bar	Struts, coils, dampers, anti-roll bar	Struts, lower wishbones, anti-roll bar
Rear suspension	MacPherson struts, coils, dampers, anti-roll bar	Multi-link, coils, dampers, anti-roll bar	Struts, coils, dampers, anti-roll bar
Steering type	Rack and pinion, power assisted	Rack and pinion, power assisted	Rack and pinion, power assisted
Lock to lock	2.3 turns	2.6 turns	2.6 turns
Front brakes	378mm ventilated discs	274mm ventilated discs	406mm ventilated discs
Rear brakes	313mm ventilated discs	284mm ventilated discs	381mm ventilated discs
Wheels	8.0Jx18in, Cast alloy	6.0Jx15in, Cast alloy	7.0Jx16in, Cast alloy
Tyres	235/40 ZR18 Michelin Pilot SX	205/60 R15 Michelin Pilot SX	205/60 R16 Bridgestone Potenza RE10

SUBARU IMPREZA

IMPREZA TURBO 5-DOOR Subaru's mighty rally-bred Impreza Turbo just keeps getting better. We put the latest purposeful, but practical, five-door model through its paces

The Subaru Impreza has always been a much underrated car. Even in basic 2.0 GL guise it has an idiosyncratic charm that its mainstream rivals lack, but it is the 4wd Turbo that has tended to dominate the headlines over the years.

It is not difficult to see why. In spirit the hot Impreza could be accused of picking up where the Lancia Integrale left off, but in reality it has grown into a more sophisticated car than the Lancia ever was, not to mention a more dynamic one.

For 1998 the focus on high performance has become sharper than ever, though not at the expense of refinement or comfort, Subaru is quick to point out. Outwardly the differences range from the fitment of larger 16in wheels and tyres and new side skirts to, most obviously, a super-aggressive front-end restyle. There are now two big driving lights integrated into the bodywork on either side of the number plate, plus a small squadron of cooling orifices carved into the bonnet.

Inside, there is a new look facia that features reasonably discreet white dials, as well as an ingenious Forester-inspired cubby on top of the

QUICK FACTS

Model	Subaru Impreza 2.0 Turbo 5dr
Price	£20,215
Top speed	143mph
0–60mph	5.5sec
30–70mph	5.6sec
60–0mph	2.6sec
MPG	19.5
For	Blinding performance, fabulous handling, seats, steering feel
Against	Frightening thirst, fidgety low speed ride, not much else

ROAD TEST

4 FEBRUARY 1998

Volume 215

No 5 | 5266

ROAD TEST IMPREZA TURBO

ACCELERATION FROM REST

True mph	seconds	speedo mph
30	1.8	32
40	3.0	43
50	4.2	54
60	5.5	64
70	7.4	74
80	9.4	85
90	12.0	95
100	15.8	106

Standing qtr mile 14.2sec/87mph
Standing km 26.7sec/120mph
30–70mph through gears 5.6sec

ACCELERATION IN GEAR

MPH	5th	4th	3rd	2nd
10–30	-	-	6.3	3.9
20–40	14.8	8.8	4.9	2.8
30–50	12.9	6.0	4.4	2.5
40–60	10.4	5.4	3.8	2.4
50–70	8.5	5.2	3.4	-
60–80	8.6	5.6	3.6	-
70–90	9.8	6.1	4.6	
80–100	11.1	6.9	-	

MAXIMUM SPEEDS

5th 143mph/5,950rpm	4th 128/7,000
3rd 90/7,000	2nd 64/7,000
1st 36/7,000	

BRAKES

30/50/70/87mph 9.1/23.8/45.0/85.3m
60–0mph 2.6sec

NOISE

Idle/max revs in 3rd 48/84dbA
30/50/70mph 66/69/72dbA

FUEL CONSUMPTION

Government figures

Urban	20.5mpg
Extra urban	34.9mpg
Combined	29.7mpg

Autocar figures

Test/touring mpg	19.5/30.2mpg
Best/worst	30.2/10.4mpg
Tank capacity	60 litres
Range	398 miles

dash. The steering wheel and gear lever now come wrapped in leather, albeit of rather thin gauge, while the deep bucket seats remain some of the finest you will find in any sporting car.

Since we last put Subaru's Integrale-basher through the road test mill, it has undergone an extensive mechanical makeover. In '97 it got a new version of the highly effective four-cylinder, turbocharged "boxer" engine in which the compression ratio was raised to an unusually high 9.5:1, thereby greatly reducing turbo lag (in theory). Alongside the modifications carried out to the pistons, inlet ports and exhaust system, this helped hike torque from 201 to 214lb ft at 4,000rpm, while power remained at an impressive 208bhp at 5,600rpm.

As a result of the alterations, the latest Impreza is little short of devastating on the road, covering ground with impressive nonchalance but at a rate which many supercars would have difficulty matching. Indeed, we can think of no other car that is quicker over the ground which also competes on price.

And even in a pure straight-line shoot-out, you will hardly find handfuls of similarly priced competitors that can match the Impreza's mighty performance. Zero to 60mph takes 5.5sec 0–100mph 15.8sec and from 30–70mph it needs

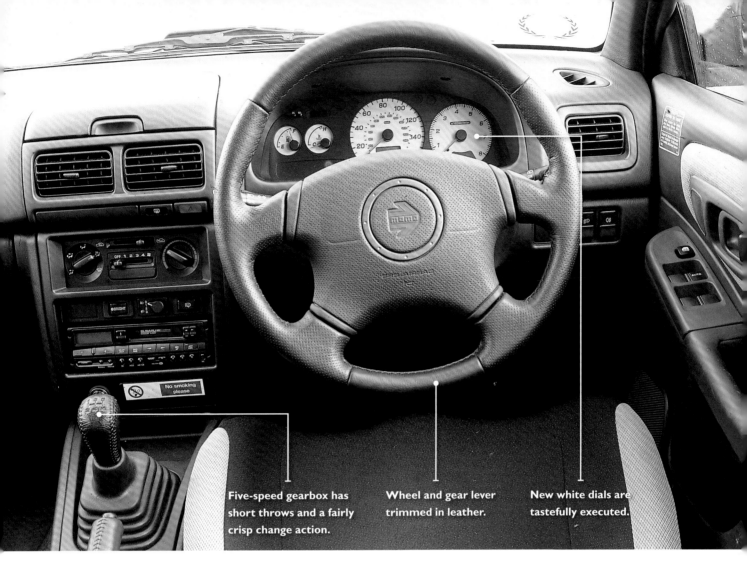

Five-speed gearbox has short throws and a fairly crisp change action.

Wheel and gear lever trimmed in leather.

New white dials are tastefully executed.

just 5.6sec – a second less than a manual Porsche Boxster. Flat out it will hit 143mph, and to get from 50–70mph in top gear it requires only 8.5sec, an amazing 5.0sec faster than before.

Just as Subaru claims, turbo lag has been all but eliminated from the throttle response, which is now as sharp as any blown car's. It also sounds a good deal fruitier than before, emitting a series of purposeful whistles and rasps that belie the car's civilised motorway gait.

We've no complaints about the strong, well weighted brakes or the excellent anti-lock system which isn't triggered until pleasingly late in the braking process. Fuel consumption, on the other hand, verges on the dreadful if you're driving quickly. Overall we managed 19.5mpg, but this dropped below 16mpg during committed use. This means you are rarely likely to get more than 300 miles out of a tank.

If it all sounds good so far, the Impreza in a straight line is as nothing compared with the Impreza in corners. Then, the combination of

LEFT Dash-top cubby and big boot are proof that Subaru thinks about practicality.

OPPOSITE Inspired chassis and 208bhp turbocharged boxer engine.

ABOVE In five-door form the Impreza Turbo is as practical as it is purposeful.

four-wheel-drive grip and traction, unusually excellent steering feel and almost immaculate body control and balance turn it into a near-uncatchable cross country missile. And if the ride is slightly compromised as a result (it's fidgety in town,

though not drastically so), then the trade-off in the form of outrageously agile open road handling is, we feel, worth it.

The fast Impreza benefits from the same quirky practicality that all versions boast. Namely, more than generous cabin room for four adults, terrific all-round frameless doors and big glass areas), good rather than top drawer build quality and, post-revamp, a perfectly decent facia with a well resolved driving position. It is not as pleasing or expensive-feeling inside as the new VW Golf, but it's at least on a par with the Peugeot 306 qualitatively and, in five-door estate form as seen here, it has a bigger boot than almost any competitor.

Combined with the blistering performance, wondrous handling balance and very real driver appeal, this blend of talents makes the Impreza Turbo a unique car in our experience. For these reasons and more it earns a full five-star rating. Last year only two cars were similarly honoured...

The best affordable performance car yet ★★★★★

WHAT IT COSTS

SUBARU IMPREZA 2.0 TURBO

On-the-road price	£20,215
Price as tested	£20,215
Cost per mile	59.9p

INSURANCE

Insurance	Group 17

WARRANTY

3 yrs/60,000 miles, 6 yrs anti-corrosion

SERVICING

Major 15,000 miles, 2.0 hours, £128
Interim 7,500 miles, 0.9 hours, £72

EQUIPMENT CHECKLIST

Anti-lock brakes	■
Metallic paint	£241
Driver/passenger airbags	■/■
Central locking/electric windows	■/■
Alloy wheels	■
Alarm/immobiliser	■/■
Radio/RDS/CD player	■/■/-
Air conditioning	£1,549
Electric sunroof	£799
Rear wash wipe	■

■ = Standard na = not available

New cabin looks classier than before, though fabulous seats are unaltered.

SPECIFICATIONS IMPREZA TURBO

DIMENSIONS

Min/max front leg room 1,110/910mm **Front head room** 980/950mm
Min/max rear leg room 630/840mm **Interior width front/rear** 1,410/1,410mm
Min/max boot width 960/1,330mm **Boot height** 410mm **Boot length** 960mm
VDA boot volume 376 litres/dm³ **Front/rear tracks** 1,465/1,450mm **Kerb weight** 1,306kg
Weight distribution front/rear 43/57 **Width** 1,690mm inc mirrors

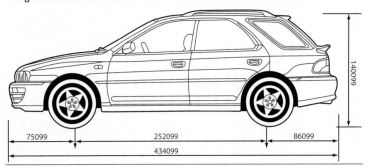

ENGINE

Layout	4 cyls, boxer, 1,994cc
Max power	208bhp/5,600rpm
Max torque	214lb ft/4,000rpm
Specific output	104bhp/litre
Power to weight	159bhp/tonne
Torque to weight	164lb ft/tonne
Installation	Front, longitudinal, four-wheel drive
Construction	Aluminium alloy head and block
Bore/stroke	92.0/75.0mm
Valve gear	4 per cyl, dohc
Compression	9.5:1
Ignition and fuel	Hitachi engine management, Hitachi turbocharger

TRANSMISSION

Gearbox 5-speed manual
Ratios/mph per 1,000rpm
Final drive 3.54

1st 3.45/5.1		**2nd** 1.95/9.1	
3rd 1.37/12.9		**4th** 0.97/18.3	
5th 0.73/24.0			

CHASSIS AND BODY

Body	5dr estate Cd 0.35
Wheels	7x16in
Made of	Alloy
Tyres	205/50 R16
Spare	Full size

STEERING

Type Rack and pinion, power assisted
Turns lock-to-lock 2.8
Turning circle 10.4m

SUSPENSION

Front MacPherson struts, coil spring/dampers, anti-roll bar
Rear Struts, coil springs/dampers, dual link, anti-roll bar

BRAKES

Front 228mm ventilated discs
Rear 230mm discs
Anti-lock Standard

The performance figures were taken at the Millbrook Proving Ground with the odometer reading 3,500 miles. *AUTOCAR* test results are protected by world copyright and may not be reproduced without the editor's written permission.

IMPREZA RB5

As an everyday road car, the latest variant of Subaru's thoroughbred, which takes its name from works team rally driver Richard Burns, is possibly the most appealing Impreza yet

The RB5 Impreza may not be the most outrageous version of Subaru's seminal four-wheel-drive giant slayer, but it is certainly one of the best. And that's saying something among company as esteemed as the eye-wateringly rapid 22B, not to mention the new WRX STi V, which is rumoured to be going on sale at regular Subaru UK dealers from the end of this year.

Should you wait until then for the ultimate Impreza? Not necessarily. The RB5, named after Subaru's new number one wheelman, Richard Burns, may not be as powerful or as quick in a straight line as the WRXs and 22Bs of this world, but as a package – and as an everyday road car it is possibly the most appealing Impreza yet.

The reasons for this are many. First, the RB5 differs from the likes of the 22B in that it is not a homologation special for rallying; it's a road car through and through. So there's no bone-jarring ride, no manic turbo lag and no "will it, won't it?" handling balance.

The RB5 starts life at the factory in Japan with a bespoke bodyshell in which the rear bulkhead is fixed (unlike normal Impreza saloons, which feature a split bulkhead to allow folding rear seats). It arrives in the UK, alongside the other 443 due for these shores, and is then handed to Prodrive, the company that prepares the works rally cars, which carries out a number of modifications.

Customers who go for the basic RB5 (price £24,995) merely get the new 17in Speedline alloy wheels, the big rear wing and the bespoke "blue steel" metallic paint job. Otherwise it's just like any other 1999 model year Impreza, with 218bhp at 5,600rpm,

QUICK FACTS

Model	Subaru Impreza RB5
Price	£27,545
On sale	Now
0–62mph	5.6sec
Top speed	141mph

NEW CARS

5 MAY 1999

Volume 220

No 5 | 5330

OPPOSITE Rally-style 17in Speedline alloys are standard; engine can be left standard or uprated by Prodrive – well worth it.

WHAT THE RB5 MUST BEAT

MAKE	AUDI	ALFA ROMEO	HONDA
Model	**S3**	**156 2.5 V6**	**Accord Type R**
Price	£26,500 (est	£22,801	£22,995
Engine	210bhp 1.8 turbo four	190bhp 2.5 V6	209bhp 2.2 four
Highlights	The quickest version of the A3 isn't quite as communicative as the Subarus of this world, but nothing can touch it at the money for quality, style and grip.	Landmark car, taking 3-series' crown for driver enjoyment. V6 engine sounds great but lacks poke here. Quick steering completes great value package.	Better even than the Integra R overall, the hot Accord is a supremely well-rounded package that gives the Impreza its biggest run for the money.

214lb ft at 4,000rpm and 0–60mph in a cool 5.6sec, according to figures extracted from our own long-term example.

The real deal, however, is this car, which is fitted with one or two other Prodrive bits, such as a quickshift gearchange and a series of engine modifications that take power to 238bhp and torque to a meaningful 258lb ft, delivered 500rpm lower than normal at 3,500rpm.

For this you must pay £27,545, but in our view it's well worth it, not least because the engine tweaks endow the Impreza with two significant advantages on the road. One, it has notably more initial response, the turbo spooling up audibly and firing the car forwards from as low as 1800rpm on full throttle. Two, the engine comes on strong again over the last 1200rpm of its rev range, which is precisely where the standard unit starts to flag. It also sounds better,

BELOW Cabin looks cheap, like that of any Impreza, but driving position is spot on; grippy seats trimmed in blue suede.

SPECIFICATIONS IMPREZA RB5

ECONOMY

Urban	20.6mpg
Extra Urban	35.3mpg
Combined	28.0mpg

DIMENSIONS

Width (exc mirrors)	1,690mm
Height	1,400mm
Wheelbase	2,520mm
Weight	1,235kg
Fuel tank	60 litres

ENGINE

Layout	4 cyls horizontally opposed, 1,994cc
Max power	238bhp at 6,000rpm
Max torque	258lb ft at 3,500rpm
Specific output	120bhp per litre
Power to weight	195bhp per tonne
Installation	Front, transverse, four-wheel drive
Made of	Aluminium alloy heads and block
Bore/stroke	92/75mm
Compression ratio	9.5:1
Valve gear	4 per cyl, dohc
Ignition and fuel	Hitachi ignition, multi-point injection, Hitachi turbocharger

GEARBOX

Type 5-speed manual by Subaru
Ratios/mph per 1,000rpm
Final drive 4.44

1st	3.17/5.1	2nd	1.89/8.6
3rd	1.30/12.4	4th	0.97/16.6
5th	0.74/21.8		

SUSPENSION

Front and rear MacPherson struts, coil springs and dampers, anti-roll bar

STEERING

Type Rack and pinion, power assisted
Turns lock-to-lock 2.7

BRAKES

Front 280mm ventilated discs
Rear 245mm ventilated discs

WHEELS AND TYRES

Size 7.0Jx17in
Made of Cast alloy
Tyres 205/45 ZR17 Pirelli P-Zero

THE AUTOCAR VERDICT

The best Impreza yet to use every day on the road. A valuable and rare jewel that is bound to appreciate in time.

throatier, at all revs thanks to the Prodrive exhaust. However, it's interesting to note that in the mid-range, particularly between 3,500 and 5,000rpm, the Prodrive lump feels more lethargic than the regular motor, which means that to get the maximum benefit you must be prepared to stir the gears a little more frantically than normal. Despite the extra weight (but shorter throw) of the quickshift gearchange, this is not exactly a hardship in the RB5.

So really what we're talking about here is a normal Impreza Turbo with bigger wheels, a tad more poke and a noisier exhaust – a less civilised but more focused model. Er, no. Somehow – and this is probably due to the extra body stiffness brought about by the rigid bulkhead – the RB5 has a better ride and feels more civilised than any Impreza Turbo we've driven. Yet through a series of corners it is more fluid and responds even more crisply to steering, throttle and brake inputs. Undoubtedly the fact that it rides on 17in 205/45 Pirelli P-Zero tyres instead of the standard car's 205/50 16in Bridgestones plays a role in sharpening its act. What you would not expect them to do is aid the ride, yet they do.

For aficionados, it will also be important to note that you get an RB5 plaque down by the gear lever, plus even more supportive seats trimmed in grippy blue suede, as well as air conditioning as standard.

But the real benefits of the RB5 can only be experienced out on the road, where it counts. Which is fitting for a car named after the great man himself.

BE IMPREZED

IMPREZA TURBO 5-DOOR Rally specials used to be famous for one thing: falling apart. But, after 25,000 hard miles, we can recommend one that doesn't

Lousy stereo. Oddly big steering wheel. No air con. Downmarket interior. No grab handle to close the boot. Excessive tyre and wind noise at motorway speeds.

Those are the 26 words that sum up what we don't like about our long-term Subaru Impreza Turbo. The remaining 1,100-odd words will lavish this ugly yet very beautiful car with little but praise.

Few other cars have been so universally popular here at *Autocar*. And after an impressive year on the long-term fleet, its last big trip offered fresh evidence of what makes the Impreza so great.

In a door-to-door race from London to Paris against the Eurostar, the Impreza was a mere 18 minutes behind the trans-Channel bullet train. Let's put that into perspective. The Eurostar can blast its way to Paris at speeds in excess of 185mph, it doesn't need to stop for fuel or load itself onto another, slower train to travel beneath the Channel.

Our Impreza faced both those obstacles but still took just nine hours and 36 minutes to cover the 1,128-mile round trip. It left photographer Barry Hayden and me refreshed and ready to go when

WHAT WE LIKE

Supercar performance, complete reliability and estate-car friendliness. Outstanding value for money. Excellent ride and brakes, negligible body roll and swift but chunky gearshift. Brilliant seats and fine driving position, hard-wearing interior and quirky styling.

WHAT WE DON'T LIKE

Performance means an extortionate appetite for petrol, tyres and clutches. Cheap-looking interior is a let down given aggressive exterior looks. Feeble stereo drowned out by excessive wind noise from frameless doors. Steering wheel too big and no air con.

IMPREZA
TURBO 2000 AWD

OUR CARS

12 JANUARY 2000

Volume 223
No 2 | 5365

AUTOCAR
FIRST FOR NEW CARS

NEW BABY
MERC
FULL STORY
SL dash for
MX-5 cash

300

THIS WEEK
FORD'S FREELANDER
IMPREZA MARATHON

NEW JAG
F-TYPE
THIS TIME IT'S FOR REAL

PLUS F1 FUTURE FIAT MULTIPLA NEW ROLLS CORNICHE

Racer tendencies need keeping in check during the running-in period

RIGHT Dealer servicing always exemplary; five door proved ideal for long trips.

we stepped out of the Impreza in Paris. It provided the perfect combination of searing performance, impeccable roadholding and a boot big enough for plenty of luggage, cameras and wine.

The train's station-to-station time from Waterloo to Gare du Nord is exactly three hours. Doing that in a car crossing the Channel by Le Shuttle would demand a McLaren F1 and a complete disregard for speed limits. But the relevant comparison must include the time it takes to get from my flat by train to the Eurostar terminus at Waterloo, check in the required 25 minutes early, and then shuffle off the Eurostar at Gare du Nord. That takes the total journey time by train to four and a half hours each way. I'll take the Impreza Express every time.

It sounded a bit of a harebrained scheme at first, taking on the Eurostar in a blast to the middle of

Paris, but it is in fact exactly the kind of challenge at which the Impreza excels, and looked certain to provide a great send-off for one of the best long termers this magazine has run.

Since it joined our fleet in November 1998, the Impreza has been in constant demand. Few cars have prompted such fierce rank-pulling on Friday afternoons. To have the Subaru for the weekend is to enjoy standards of performance and roadholding, irrespective of destination or weather conditions, that until recently were associated more often with the likes of Porsche and Ferrari.

Its ability to chew up and spit out any fastlane pretender is made even more enjoyable by its oddball styling, which owes more to a warthog than a wind tunnel, and a transmission superbly matched to the engine.

We opted for the less popular estate version, predicting – rightly – that its five doors would make it better suited than the saloon to the varied demands of life on the *Autocar* fleet.

Although the 1,000-mile run-in period limiting the engine to 4,000rpm proved frustrating for the first owner of the keys, Hugo Andreae, it was clear from the off that the performance was going to be a revelation and that life after a £21,450 estate that zips to 60mph in 5.3sec would never be the same.

Winter excursions to Wales and Wiltshire showed the ease with which the Impreza's four-wheel drive system, equipped with a limited-slip differential, copes with icy roads and muddy farm tracks.

Then last March we pitted the Impreza against the Audi S3. Despite the similarities – a hatch at the back, all-wheel drive and

Door-to-door journey by Eurostar was barely any quicker and much less fun than using Impreza

IMPREZA TURBO

Car run for 13 months
Introduced in UK March 1994
Changes since then October '97: interior styling revised and torque up from 201lb ft at 4,800rpm to 214lb ft at 4,000rpm. October '98: saloon gets higher rear wing and power rises from 208bhp to 215bhp.
What makes it special? World's best-preserved five-year-old has raspy turbo-blown flat four which is unique to Subaru. Rally bred all-wheel drive and limited-sLip differential also found in fearsome WRX and 22B variants. Bland interior lifted by chunky Momo wheel and bucket seats. Oddball styling gives hatchback versatility.

BELOW Impreza adds to attraction in Paris; steering wheel too big for full sporty effect.

LOGBOOK IMPREZA TURBO

TEST STARTED 1.11.98

Mileage at start	150
Mileage now	26,277

PRICES

List price new		£21,450
Metallic paint option		£241
Total price with options		£21,691
Value now:	Trade	£15,300
	Private	£16,000
	Retail	£16,750

FUEL CONSUMPTION

Govt urban	20.6mpg
Extra urban	35.3mpg
Combined	28.0mpg
Our test best	29.5mpg
Our test worst	17.3mpg
Our test average	22.9mpg

PERFORMANCE

0–30mph	1.8sec
0–40mph	3.0sec
0–50mph	4.2sec
0–60mph	5.3sec
0–70mph	7.4sec
0–80mph	9.4sec
Standing qtr mile	14.2sec/87mph
Standing km	26.7sec/120mph
Top speed	143mph

SERVICING AND TYRES

1,000 miles
Change oil and filter £46.21
7,500 miles
Change oil and filter £104.22
15,000 miles
Change oil and filter, new
front brake pads and clutch £336.67
22,000 miles
Change oil and filter £110.73

PARTS COSTS

Complete front bumper £294.58, headlamp £154.34, door mirror £105.49, windscreen £197.68, alloy wheel without tyre £314.84 (inc VAT)

TYRES

205/50 ZR16 Bridgestone Potenza £166.50 each (inc VAT and fitting)

FAULTS

5,000 miles Intermittent problems with remote locking fob
13,500 miles New tyres fitted
15,000 miles New clutch under warranty
17,000 miles Gearshift intermittently reluctant to engage. Indicators failed
24,000 miles New tyres fitted

COSTS OVER 26,000 MILES

Fuel	£3861.81
Oil (non service)	None
Service and parts	£375.01
Tyres	£1,332
Repairs	None
Total running costs	£5,791.64
Running costs per mile	22p
Cost per mile (incl depreciation)	46.36p

INSURANCE

25-year-old man, single, two speeding fines, five years' no-claims bonus, living in high-risk Manchester (£200 excess) **£1,033.77**
35-year-old man, married, clean licence, five years' no-claims bonus, in low-risk Swindon with garage (£200 excess) **£576.90**

Quotes from What Car? Insurance

FINAL VIEW

The Impreza Turbo is an icon of the '90s. Driving any other car after the Impreza always serves to highlight the Subaru's phenomenal speed and awesome handling. No wonder the rally cars continue to score highly. Now the next-generation Impreza Turbo is eagerly awaited.

Previous reports: 18.11.98, 3.2.99, 7.4.99, 21.7.99, 15.9.99

storming acceleration from turbocharged four-cylinder engines, each pushing out over 200bhp – the quirky Impreza emerged triumphant with far sharper dynamic rewards.

But the S3 highlights the Imprezas weaknesses. The Audi's stylish and well-built cabin makes a mockery of the Subaru's bland, plasticky cockpit. The Impreza's steering wheel seems too large and the stereo is pathetic. The frameless doors mean wind noise is often intrusive at motorway speeds. And the arthritic windows always give the impression they will never fully open and close, although in fact they do always stutter to their destination.

The Impreza is a make-mine-a-double dipsomaniac, as our average fuel consumption figure of 22.89mpg suggests. On one trip to France it guzzled a gallon of unleaded every 12 miles. It never bettered 30mpg in our hands. Two sets of tyres – the fabulous 205/50 ZR16 Bridgestone Potenzas that took top honours our tyre test last year – also dented the wallet by £650.

In July, we complained of a truculent gearchange, prompting a reader to tip us off about an uprated clutch. We duly had ours replaced under warranty and the problem went away.

Servicing the Impreza was an equally painless

affair. It was carried out by Ace Kensington – Subaru's only dealer in London – and Bell and Colvill in Surrey, and both dealerships provided nothing but quick and effective work. The Impreza was always returned to us washed and scrubbed inside and out.

Giving a passenger their first ride in the Impreza is always an entertaining experience for the driver, and often an enlightening one for the passenger. One friend of mine sniffed sceptically at the Subaru, made a disparaging comment about its overwhelming ugliness and snorted at its interior.

But a full-throttle take-off and a blast down my favourite B-road soon convinced him of the error of his ways. Like most passengers, he got out of the car in awe-struck silence, pointed at the bonnet and asked in hushed tones what lurked beneath it.

The sheer quantity of power on tap makes the Subaru highly addictive. Arcade-game acceleration is there in any gear at any speed on any road. Throttle-adjustable cornering attitude, oversteer, four-wheel drifting – they're all there to reward the dedicated driver.

Since we ran our first long-term Impreza Turbo in 1994, the car has single-handedly turned Subaru from a little-known maker of odd-looking cars into an icon-builder. Backed by its success in the World Rally Championship, the Impreza Turbo has become to the '90s what the Peugeot 205 GTi was to the '80s.

It has redefined the way we judge cars, a feat summed up by the final entry in the logbook. It reads simply: "I am so glad I got to drive this car."

Striking Subaru always attracts plenty of attention – sometimes too much

OPPOSITE Rail users need to queue for a taxi at Waterloo; it won't be an Impreza.

ABOVE Time for a quick wash and brush-up.

'THE SHEER QUANTITY OF POWER ON TAP MAKES THE SUBARU HIGHLY ADDICTIVE'

SUBARU IMPREZA P1

Prodrive's brief: the definitive Impreza Turbo, crafted to suit UK roads. So no more grey imports, no more crude Japanese conversions, no more excuses. It's crunch time

The wait is over. Welcome to the Subaru Impreza P1 the latest and most eagerly awaited rally-derived road burner for the year 2000.

For all the standard Impreza Turbo's undeniable talent, and the performance upgrades available from Prodrive, it has been difficult for Subaru UK and punters alike not to acknowledge yet faster variations of the car intended for Japanese consumption but shipped to the UK as grey imports.

Best of the lot is the WRX STi three-door: a 280bhp homologation special with uprated brakes and a stiffer bodyshell. Just the car then, for Subaru to import and sell in small numbers.

But that wasn't the aim of this exercise. Merely import an existing model and you end up competing with hundreds of independent car traders doing exactly the same thing. A unique UK flagship based on the WRX was needed. A car developed and type approved on our roads to be sold as a model in its own right through Subaru UK's regular dealerships.

That's exactly what the P1 is. A machine created out of the WRX, but shorn of many rough edges to maximise its potential as everyday transport.

DESIGN AND ENGINEERING ★★★★
Developed in the UK for the UK market

So sound is the blend of performance, refinement and value in the standard Impreza Turbo that we've always considered it to be a better road car than the WRX.

There was only one place for Subaru to turn for the expertise required to tame such a car: Prodrive. The P1 is intended to be the first in a succession of limited edition models developed by the Banbury-based outfit with more Scooby sense than anyone outside the Subaru factory itself.

The decision to type approve a new model was driven by both marketing and engineering needs. The execution of such a project has been an uphill struggle that exposes the vast chasm that exists between Japanese and European production regulations.

The biggest hurdle for Prodrive was modifying the 1994cc horizontally opposed turbo engine to comply with European noise and emissions requirements while retaining the standard WRX's 277bhp. Top of the list of changes was a reprogrammed electronic control unit designed and manufactured by Fuji. A new catalytic converter has been fitted, the standard twin catalysts being ditched for a larger single item.

The result is a cleaner and quieter engine, but one that loses none of the WRX's outright poke. Maximum power is an identical 277bhp at 6,500rpm, while peak torque stays at 253lb ft at 4,000rpm.

Subaru UK has never sold the two-door Impreza, so the car needed European type approval. Months of legal wrangles and miles of red tape later, complete bodyshells that meet all European safety demands are now leaving the factory in Japan with a solid rear bulkhead for greater structural rigidity. Twin airbags are also standard.

So large is Subaru Technica International's (STi) range of springs and dampers that Prodrive tried no less than 22 variations. In standard spec the WRX

QUICK FACTS

Model tested	Subaru Impreza P1
List price	£31,495
Top speed	155mph
30–70mph	4.8sec
0–60mph	4.7sec
60–0mph	2.5sec
MPG	19.5
For	Rock hard looks, performance, stunning ride quality
Against	Weak brakes, numb steering

ROAD TEST

5 APRIL 2000

Volume 224

No 1 | 5377

NEW LOOK!

AUTOCAR

They call it the ultimate. Find out why we don't

IMPREZA P1 FIRST DRIVE

800

PLUS EVO VI SHOOTOUT

FIRST PICTURES NEW CORSA

FIRST UK DRIVE SPORT CLIO

PLUS TOURING CAR STARS GO MAD IN YORKSHIRE

W873 JDA

ABOVE Ride and compliance are exemplary, with even the lumpiest roads tamed by the PI. But the pay-off comes in reduced driver satisfaction and feedback.

OPPOSITE Strut brace betrays PI's STi roots; rear spoiler unique to PI, offering aerodynamic advantages and added visual agression.

is too harsh for UK roads, so the PI retains the WRX's rear springs but uses softer front springs and uprated dampers all round to achieve a more compliant ride.

The key is revised front and rear geometry with particular attention being paid to tyre choice. Prodrive's competition relationship with Pirelli has helped the chassis engineers develop a car that uses 17 rather than 16in alloy wheels and lower profile 205/45 P-Zero tyres (the WRX uses 205/50S).

HISTORY

Subaru UK is keen to play down any connection the PI has with other Subarus, but eagle-eyed Scooby fans will spot that the bodyshell is from the latest WRX STi three-door. Prodrive has offered tuning kits for the Impreza for some time now, and in 1998 developed the 240bhp WR Prodrive. Later that year came the 22B, a wide-bodied monster we felt was too harsh for the road. Best of the lot was the RB5, a 240bhp WR Prodrive liveried to celebrate Richard Burns's continued rally success.

Dynamic excellence needed to be matched by a bespoke look. Peter Stevens of McLaren F1 fame restyled key areas of the body; the most striking aspect is the lack of gold wheels. Subaru has called time on such extravagance and the new OZ rims are gunmetal grey, in anticipation of the world rally car using the same for the rest of the season. The front and rear spoilers are unique to the PI and offer aerodynamic advantages over the obvious added visual aggression. Tests show the PI requires 3bhp less to maintain 100mph than the standard car.

Demand has been strong enough for Subaru to double the total production run from 500 to 1000 units. They are all sold.

PERFORMANCE/BRAKES ★★★★
Stunning performance, lacklustre brakes

Just a quick glance at the PI's specification tells you all you need to know about the car's performance. Anything that has 277bhp in a body weighing 1,283kg is going to be swift. And the PI does not disappoint.

Nothing gets off the line like a turbocharged four-wheel-drive car. Full revs, sidestep the clutch and the resultant burst of acceleration almost beggars belief.

ROAD TEST IMPREZA P1

MAXIMUM SPEEDS
5th 155mph/7,500rpm 4th 133/8,200
3rd 96/8,200   2nd 66/8,200
1st 39/8,200

ACCELERATION FROM REST

True mph	seconds	speedo mph
30	1.6	33
40	2.5	44
50	3.6	54
60	4.7	65
70	6.4	76
80	8.0	86
90	9.8	97
100	12.3	108

Standing qtr mile 13.9sec/105mph
Standing km 24.6sec/127mph
30–70mph through gears 4.8sec

ACCELERATION IN GEAR

MPH	5th	4th	3rd	2nd
20–40	12.7	7.8	4.9	2.7
30–50	10.9	5.9	3.6	2.1
40–60	8.8	4.4	3.0	2.2
50–70	6.8	3.9	2.9	-
60–80	5.7	4.0	3.3	-
70–90	6.1	4.4	4.0	-
80–100	6.5	5.0	-	-

BRAKES
30/50/70mph 9.6/24.9/46.3 metres
60–0mph 2.5sec

NOISE
Idle/max revs in 3rd 54/78dbA
30/50/70mph 68/70/73dbA

FUEL CONSUMPTION
Average/best/worst/touring
19.5/25.9/9.9/25.9mpg

Urban	19.2mpg
Extra urban	31.0mpg
Combined	25.2mpg
Tank capacity	60 litres
Touring range	340 miles

TESTER'S NOTES
Everywhere we went in Wales, people recognised the P1 as something a bit special. This side of the Severn bridge it just faded into the swelling ranks of hot Imprezas. It still looks tough enough for us, though.

The VDO stereo fitted to the test car deserves a special mention for being the fiddliest unit we have ever tried. No knobs, no preset numbers, and an array of warning beeps. What is the in-car hi-fi world coming to?

Rally ace Richard Burns won't have much time to pootle around in the company P1 – he's just bought a 911 GT3. Good though the Scooby may be, we'd take the Porsche on all but the wettest days.

The 205/45 Pirelli P-Zero tyres are an unusual size developed specially for P1, but they will soon be available for any car. For ride and refinement they are unbeatable.

While you're looking for the locomotive that feels like it's just walloped you up the backside, the computer is trying hard to keep up with a string of figures that reads 0–30mph in 1.6sec, 0–60mph in 4.7sec and an effortless 12.4sec to 100mph.

Boost builds very quickly between 2,000–3,000rpm, at which point the benefits of a properly sorted forced-induction engine leap sharply into focus. From here the engine undergoes a delicious change of character. That friendly trademark Subaru warble rises an octave and then screams all the way to the 8,200rpm limiter. The sheer energy with which it slices through the last 2,000rpm is especially impressive for a unit that delivers its peak power at 6,500rpm.

It's not all top end, though. Leave the P1 in fourth and it romps from 30–50mph in just 5.9sec, pulling off a similar trick between 50–70mph in top – it takes 6.8sec. Mighty impressive stuff from just 2.0 litres.

The gearshift – STi rather than Prodrive-derived – is also excellent and the ratios are well suited to UK roads. We can verify that 155mph maximum speed too, and the inherent stability provided by the body addenda at such speeds.

But once again the Mitsubish Evo VI GSR proves to be the thorn in the Subaru's seemingly

WHAT IT COSTS

SUBARU IMPREZA WRX

On-the-road price	£31,495
Price as tested	£31,495

INSURANCE

Insurance/typical quote	20/£2,100

WARRANTY

36 months/60,000 miles, 6 years rust

SERVICING

Major 15,000 miles
Minor 7,500 miles

EQUIPMENT CHECKLIST

Air conditioning	■
Traction control	na
Leather trim	na
Height/tilt-adjust steering columm	na/■
Anti-lock brakes	■
Airbag driver/passenger	■/■
Satellite navigation	na
Alarm/immobiliser	■/■
RDS stereo/CD player	■/■

■ = Standard na = not available

BELOW Prodrive has developed the P1 to have ultimate mix of familiar Impreza performance with new ride refinement.

impregnable armour. Taking how brisk the P1 felt during our session at Millbrook, the Evo's 0–60mph and 0–100mph times of 4.4sec and 11.2sec seem outrageous. It's the same story in the gears too. The Mitsubishi shaves 0.9sec off the P1's fourth gear time and a whole second off its fifth gear time.

We can't repeat such praise for the braking system. Frankly, we expected more from the P1 –

more pedal feel and more resistance to fade. Pushed to extremes –'but not too often – they deliver the goods, hence our 2.5sec 60–0mph time. But ask too much and they respond with substantial fade and, in some cases, clouds of smoke.

HANDLING AND RIDE ★★★★
Great ride, pity about the slow steering

Subaru had a clear objective in mind when it commissioned Prodrive to develop the P1. That it would have massive grip and traction went without saying. The critical ingredient deemed necessary for the British market was ride refinement.

No other Japanese high-performance car of this type comes close to matching it in this area. Trawling through town over potholes, the P1 feels as compliant as a BMW 3-series. Add some speed to the equation and it just gets better.

The P1 has a rare ability to smooth surfaces a driver's eye has marked down as being potentially troublesome. Under the same conditions a WRX would be an uncomfortable handful and even the standard Impreza Turbo wouldn't settle in the same manner.

But a handling and ride combination is a compromise, so something had to give. In the case of the P1, satisfaction and feedback have been forced to take a back seat.

Prodrive considered fitting a quicker steering rack to the car, but found the combination of that rack and the softer new front end made the car too nervous. So the P1 makes do with the standard Impreza rack, which takes 2.7 turns lock to lock, and loses a crucial degree of manoeuvrability. Challenging sections of B-road that should require nothing more than half a turn of lock in either direction need a couple of extra degrees. It's a small difference, but enough to mar the fun.

The other slight blot in the copybook is the P1's less than dogged resistance to understeer. We're used to Imprezas amazing us with awesome front-end grip, but the P1's front 205/45 ZR17 Pirelli P-Zeros start to slither earlier than expected. Perhaps the biggest disappointment is not being able to deal with the understeer by adding to or cutting the throttle.

What emerges is a chassis that is not the last word in driver involvement, rather one that's built for those who will use the P1 as everyday transport. What it loses to the Evo on a 50-mile blast over the

Pennines, it recoups by dealing with all the M1 can throw at it in four hours. But the driving experience has suffered because of it.

SAFETY AND EQUIPMENT ★★★★
Still practical, even as a two-door

This is the area that has traditionally tended to throw the conventional supercar establishment into deep confusion. Japanese performance cars like this aren't just capable of destroying machinery costing twice the money cross-country, they can also offer ample space for four adults, as well as a large boot.

The recipe for the P1 is little different to any other Impreza *Autocar* has tested except for its lack of rear doors. The boot is exactly the same size as the four-door's. Front passengers get by far the best deal and sit in superb Prodrive bucket seats. It's difficult to think of road car chairs that offer the same combination of lateral support and long-distance comfort. The driving position is spot on, with the distance between the steering wheel and pedals proving comfortable for everyone who drove the car.

Had the P1 turned out to be a pared-to-the-bones racer, it might have been easier to excuse

ABOVE Supremely comfortable bucket seats give occupants superb back support.

SPECIFICATIONS IMPREZA P1

DIMENSIONS

Min/max front leg room 910/1,110mm Min/max rear leg room 630/840mm
Min/max front head room 930/980mm Interior width front/rear 1,410/1,410mm
Boot length 960mm Boot height 380mm Min/max boot width 960/1,330mm
VDA boot volume 365 litres/dm³ Front/rear tracks 1,459mm/1,449mm
Kerb weight 1,283kg Weight distribution front/rear 60/40 Width 1,920mm inc mirrors

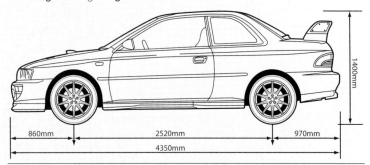

860mm 2520mm 970mm 4350mm 1400mm

ABOVE Front scoops
direct cooling air to brakes.

BELOW Bespoke 7x17in OZ
alloy wheels were designed by
Peter Stevens. They look superb
but are a nightmare to clean.

ENGINE

Layout	4 cyls, 1,994cc
Max power	277bhp at 6,500pm
Max torque	253lb ft at 4,000rpm
Power to weight	215bhp per tonne
Torque to weight	197lb ft per tonne
Installation	Front, transverse, four- wheel drive
Construction	Alloy heads and block
Bore/stroke	92.0/75.0mm
Valve gear	4 valves per cylinder, dohc per bank
Compression	ratio 8.2:1
Ignition and fuel	Hitachi ignition, sequential fuel injection, Hitachi turbo with intercooler

TRANSMISSION

Gearbox	5-speed manual
Ratios/mph per 1,000rpm	
Final drive	4.44

1st	3.17/4.8	2nd	1.88/8.1
3rd	1.30/11.7	4th	0.97/16.2
5th	0.74/20.6		

CHASSIS AND BODY

Body	2 door saloon
Wheels	7Jx17in
Made of	Alloy
Tyres	205/45 ZR 17 Pirelli P-Zero
Spare	Full size

STEERING

Type	Rack and pinion, power assisted
Turns lock-to-lock	2.7
Turning circle	10.4m

SUSPENSION

Front MacPherson struts, lower wishbones, coil springs, anti-roll bar
Rear MacPherson struts, coil springs, anti-roll bar

BRAKES

Front 280mm ventilated discs
Rear 245mm ventilated discs
Anti-lock Standard

ECONOMY ★★★★
Loves guzzling but can be surprisingly frugal

The fuel figures start to look like they should come from a much larger engine than the P1's 1994cc if you keep your right foot to the carpet. At the track we recorded 9.9mpg, and our poor 19.5mpg test average included some sedate cruising.

Use a lighter right foot, and you might equal our 25.2mpg touring figure. Easier said than done once you've heard the engine at 7000rpm. At best, 342 miles is available between fill-ups of super unleaded.

MARKET AND FINANCE ★★★★
Full UK back-up and they're all sold already

Over the past five years the Impreza Turbo has built a brilliant reputation for reliability and rock-solid residuals. It was one of the few cars that worked as a rational as well as an emotional purchase.

The situation has weakened a little over the past six months but that won't affect the P1.

Each of the 1000 examples due to be produced has found a home and a reserve waiting list has been started.

Being an official Subaru model does wonders for the P1's reputation on the market. The £31,495 price isn't cheap, but the specification is high and no-one can argue with a comprehensive three-year, 60,000-mile warranty.

the lack of style and quality that pervades the entire cabin. The controls work well enough, but for £31,495 something more than the hard plastics that are barely palatable in a standard £20,000 Impreza are expected.

Here is where the P1's superb ride pays dividends. It really is a car in which long journeys are no hassle whatsoever. Wind and engine noise are kept well in check, and tyre and suspension thump are all but non-existent.

Standard equipment is typically generous, with electric windows, central locking, a Thatcham-approved alarm and immobiliser and air con all fitted as standard.

Safety is one of the P1's best assets. Both front seat occupants have an airbag, and anti-lock is standard. But it's the high levels of active safety inherent in a fast four-wheel-drive car that help the P1 score well. In our eyes, all that grip and power leaves it better qualified than most to avoid accidents in the first place.

AUTOCAR VERDICT

Is the P1 the ultimate road car, or even just the ultimate Impreza? The answer is not quite.

At its unveiling Subaru and Prodrive made no secret that this car was designed to fulfil two briefs. First, it was to be the best Impreza ever on the road. Second, it would wrest the cross-country crown from the fearsome Mitsubishi Evo VI.

In our view it succeeds on neither front. The P1 is definitely faster than the Turbo and the RB5. But it is questionable whether it's any more fun.

There's little point trying to hide our disappointment with the brakes and steering. It's a real pity the brakes weren't developed to match the rest of the car dynamically. As for the steering, it's a case of what might have been.

In isolation the P1 is a shatteringly impressive car, one whose body control and suspension composure set new hot saloon standards. But it is not the mould-breaker we had expected. Perhaps we expected too much.

Not the Impreza masterclass we expected ★★★★

P SHOOTER

IMPREZA P1 WORLD RALLY Stuff Euro regulation, says Prodrive. The result is what the fearsome P1 should have been first time around. Stephen Sutcliffe reports

Snow chains. Believe it or not, they're probably the main reason why the Subaru Impreza P1 never quite turned out to be the car it could have been.

You remember the P1, the ultimate version of the ultimate car. That was the theory, at any rate. But in practice, because Subaru and Prodrive were so determined to make the P1 achieve full European type approval to make it part of the regular family line-up, certain aspects of the design had to be compromised slightly. Like the wheel and tyre sizes.

Confused? Then allow me to explain. With 17-inch wheels you can still just about squeeze a set of snow chains onto an Impreza, which is one of the things stipulated by European whole vehicle type approval. But with 18-inch wheels the dreaded chains won't fit. So despite the fact that Prodrive knew the P1 would ride, handle and even steer better on 18-inch wheels, in the end it produced the car with 17-inch rims and chewed its bottom lip.

Result? The P1 got full Euro approval, unlike the hordes of grey import WRXs and Colt Car Company Mitsubishi Evos that roam our roads. But it wasn't as focused a machine as Prodrive would have liked.

So enter, six months later, the P1 World Rally – the car Prodrive would almost certainly have produced had it been liberated from the (snow) chains of European legislation. Now that the P1 has got its Euro passport, you see, things like larger wheels can be added to the specification under the pseudonym of "dealer fit options". Get it?

The differences between a P1 WR and a regular P1 are not huge, it must be said. But they're enough to turn an already brilliant high-performance road car into one that touches genius. And by that I mean one that is good enough to stand proud of any Evo VI you'd care to compare it with, so long as you don't mention things like price or acceleration too loudly.

What's the point in offering an upgraded version of a car that's already sold out in this country? Well, this is where it gets interesting, particularly if you're already the owner of a P1 and fancy adding yet more spice to your life. All the modifications that differentiate a P1 WR from a regular P1 can be ordered from, and fitted by, Prodrive right now. Cumulatively or individually.

These are, in no particular order: taller and fatter 7.5x18in OZ wheels with ultra low-profile 225/35 Pirelli P-Zero rubber, bigger and better four-pot Alcon front brake calipers and discs, a fruity new exhaust, two of the best front seats you'll ever sit in, plus a pair of gas discharge headlamps that are good enough to illuminate entire continents.

The only snag is the price. But if you bought a P1 in the first place you won't be someone who is maniacally price conscious. And if you are, why didn't you buy an Evo instead?

The brakes alone cost £1,527.50, the 18-inch wheel and tyre upgrades a further £1,980. But between them they make a big difference to the way the P1 behaves. Throw in £380 of exhaust, £1995 for the superb electric Recaro seats and £470 for the firestarter headlights and you're looking at £6,352.50 on top of the £31,495 for a basic P1.

If the words taking and Mickey spring to mind, then bear this in mind: Audi is about to put the RS4 estate on sale at 10 grand more. It's neither as fast nor as much fun as the WR. Nor, in my eyes, as knee

QUICK FACTS

Model	Subaru Impreza P1 World Rally
Price	£37,847
On sale in UK	Now
0–60mph	4.7sec
30–70mph	4.8sec
30–50mph in 4th	5.9sec
50–70mph in top	6.8sec
Standing quarter	13.9sec/105mph
Standing km	24.6sec/127mph
60–0mph	2.5sec
Top speed	155mph

FEATURE

16 AUGUST 2000

Volume 225

No 7 | 5396

SPECIFICATIONS P1 WR

ECONOMY
Best/worst	26.2/13.6mpg

DIMENSIONS
Length	4,350mm
Width	1,920mm
Height	1,400mm
Wheelbase	2,520mm
Weight	1,285kg
Fuel tank	60 litres

ENGINE
Layout	4 cyls, boxer, 1,994cc
Max power	277bhp at 6,500rpm
Max torque	260lb ft at 4,000rpm
Specific output	139bhp per litre
Power to weight	216bhp per tonne
Torque to weight	196lb ft per tonne
Installation	Front, transverse, four-wheel drive
Bore/stroke	92.0/75.0mm
Made of	Cast alloy heads and block
Compression ratio	8.2:1
Valve gear	4 per cylinder, dohc
Ignition and fuel	Hitachi ignition, sequential fuel injection

All figures are manufacturer's claims, except those relating to weight and performance

GEARBOX
Type 6-speed manual by STi
Ratios/mph per 1,000rpm

1st	3.17/5.1	2nd	1.88/8.6
3rd	1.30/12.4	4th	0.97/16.7
5th	0.74/21.9		

SUSPENSION
Front Struts, coil springs, anti-roll bar
Rear Struts, coil springs, anti-roll bar

STEERING
Type Rack and pinion, power assisted
Turns lock-to-lock 2.7

BRAKES
Front 330mm ventilated discs
Rear 245mm ventilated discs
Anti lock Standard

WHEELS AND TYRES
Size 7.5Jx18in
Made of Cast alloy
Tyres 225/35 ZR18 Pirelli P-Zero

THE **AUTOCAR** VERDICT
The most focused Impreza yet. And the first car to make the Evo VI look flawed.

tremblingly good looking. Our long-term test Evo VI RSX costs 10 grand less. But then again, it feels like it does, especially inside.

All your natural instincts tell you that a car with lower profile and bigger diameter tyres should not ride as well as the standard item, but in practice the opposite is true. In fact the new tyres eradicate most of the niggling doubts about the regular P1 on their own.

The WR now slices into corners as aggressively as you could wish for, without the nagging understeer that occasionally blunts the ordinary version. And the ride is just incredible. You watch ruts looming towards you in the road, assuming they're going to send a great crash through the car's frame. But just at the moment when you think the impact is going to occur the WR does something extraordinary and simply absorbs the intrusion like it was no more than an empty packet of fags. No steering kickback, no shudder through the chassis, no contest with an Evo VI, whose ride is simply not in the same league as this.

And that's how the WR feels throughout. More refined, more grown-up, more relevant as an everyday car than the manic Mitsubishi.

But what's most encouraging is that although the differences between this car and the regular P1 are small, together they give it that extra raw edge which allows you not to feel short-changed on the thrills front beside the Evo VI. In standard form the P1 is perhaps a tad too sensible for its own good, but in this guise, with the rorty exhaust and hip-hugging seats, it delves that little bit further into your imagination.

And as for the brakes, they're just awesome. Okay, you get the odd chirp of pad squeal around town, but when you stand on them properly for the first time it's how you imagine a jet fighter would feel landing on an aircraft carrier. You stop. Straight away.

What's more, they're not of the "stand on them gently and get thrown through the windscreen" variety. There is real feel beneath your right foot, the like of which only Porsche has ever managed to replicate consistently over the years.

Prodrive also claims that the new exhaust liberates a teeny bit more mid-range excitement from the 2.0-litre turbo engine, though it doesn't claim any more outright power than the regular P1. Even so, 277bhp

at 6,500rpm and 260lb ft at 4000rpm are still enough to make it feel blisteringly rapid on the road. Maybe not as explosive as an Evo below 3,500rpm but at least as fast in the mid-range and possibly even barmier between 6,000–8,000rpm.

It sounds better than an Evo, too, the new exhaust amplifying the boxer engine's distinctive thrum to a point where it makes a delicious noise, though never intrusively so. You even get the odd pop and crackle on over-run, just like a WRC car.

It's this sort of fine judgement that makes the WR such a compellingly great car, more so than the regular P1 – and by some margin. It's thrilling without being overly tiresome on an everyday basis, ridiculously fast yet in no way frantic. In many ways it's the car for people who have grown out of their Evos and WRXs but can't bear the thought of driving something ordinary.

Now that Subaru in Japan is finally starting to take real notice of the things Prodrive can achieve on the road as well as on the special stage, things from Prodrive can only get better in the future. On the evidence of this car it could be the start of something truly significant.

ABOVE Prodrive's modifications add a touch of genius to the P1. Excellent handing, super-smooth ride and awesome brakes offer the ultimate road-going drive.

ICON AND ON AND ON

IMPREZA WRX How do you replace a car that could do no wrong? With caution, thinks Subaru. Most changes in the new Impreza are intelligent but subtle. *By Keith Howard*

Subaru's amazing metamorphosis from farmyard mud-plugger to rally giant and purveyor of bargain supercars is down to one model: the Impreza Turbo. Introduced in 1994, in a few short years it propelled itself to a unique place in the affections of car enthusiasts, particularly in the UK. And no wonder – for repmobile money it offered all-weather performance virtually unmatched at any price.

Subaru and parent company Fuji Heavy Industries were as surprised and delighted as anyone at the transformation, but success is a double-edged sword. Sooner or later even landmark cars have to be replaced and it's inevitably a tightrope walk.

For its all-new Turbo WRX, already on sale in Japan and due in the UK in November, Subaru has attempted a difficult combination: to create a more refined, grown-up car that retains the competition-inspired edge to its performance and handling. If this can be achieved there's no reason why the legend that put Subaru on the map can't continue to blossom.

STYLING AND DESIGN

The styling of the new car elicits mixed reactions. There's no doubting it is cleaner and more modern, but it's arguably a tad staid. Subaru's response is that it would rather create a look that gradually grows on people rather than one which knocks them dead but ages rapidly.

Ignore early pictures you may have seen of the car without its chin spoiler and the saloon's rear deck spoiler. Although Subaru in Japan was originally intending not to incorporate the latter, Subaru UK insisted on it as an essential part of the car's image. Styling cues carried over from the old model are mostly clustered round the front end: the trademark

"dinner plate" fog lamps on either side of the large inlet grille and, on the Turbo WRX, the distinctive bonnet air scoop.

All new Imprezas – including the normally aspirated 1.6 and 2.0-litre variants – are available as before in two body styles: either four-door saloon (there's no longer a two-door) or five-door estate (or "sports wagon"). Both have improved interiors, with superior materials and enhanced tactile quality for the controls. The Impreza is still no Audi in this respect but it's a major step forward.

Improved packaging has allowed an increase in interior space without adding much to the car's external dimensions. Overall length is up by just 65mm and height by 35mm in the saloon, 60mm in the estate. Interior width has improved by 21mm and headroom by over 30mm, with the estate's rear leg room increased by 71mm. A new height-adjustable seat and larger range of steering wheel tilt improve comfort up front.

Load carrying capability is enhanced as a result of the saloon's wider opening bootlid and the estate's revised rear seat which now folds completely flat.

Traditionally reluctant to quote aerodynamic figures, Subaru claims an unexceptional drag coefficient of 0.32 for the estate. No figure is offered for the saloon but as the two variants' quoted top speeds are similar – 143mph for the saloon, 140mph for the estate – there can't be much in it.

ENGINE AND TRANSMISSION

One of the key ingredients of the old Impreza's recipe was its four-pot horizontally opposed boxer engine – a powerplant as unlike the wheezy old Beetle boxer as you could imagine but with the same advantages of good inherent dynamic balance

'ALL THE SIGNS POINT TO A MORE REFINED,
GROWN UP IMPREZA TURBO'

FEATURE

18 OCTOBER 2000

Volume 226

No 3 | 5405

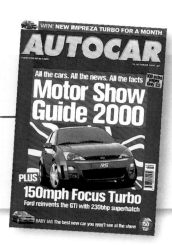

WIN! NEW IMPREZA TURBO FOR A MONTH

AUTOCAR

All the cars. All the news. All the facts

Motor Show Guide 2000

PLUS

150mph Focus Turbo

Ford reinvents the GTi with 230bhp superhatch

BABY JAG The best new car you won't see at the show

(and hence refinement) and a low centre of gravity to assist handling. Nobody wanted to see this characterful powerplant and its distinctive engine note abandoned, but there will be disappointment that Subaru hasn't done more to uprate it.

In spite of the fact that, due principally to the enhanced stiffness and crashworthiness of its bodyshell, the new car's kerb weight has increased by over 100kg, outputs remain much as before. Contrary to some early reports, the IHI turbo is not bigger – although the intercooler is, by 11 per cent – and there has been no increase in maximum power, which remains 215bhp (a specific output of 108bhp per litre). Peak torque is up and is now developed 400rpm lower at 3,600rpm, but overlay the torque curves of the old and new engines and you'll find there's barely daylight between them. In fact, the peak torque figure has increased by just 1lb ft to 215.4lb ft – nowhere near enough to offset that weight increase. Subaru isn't specific about where this small improvement originates, but changes to the inlet system are the probable source.

As a result the new car is not as accelerative as the old model, although a 5.9sec 0–60mph time is claimed. The old five-door model, which weighed just 1,235kg, recorded a 0–60mph time of 5.3sec and 0–100mph in 14.9sec. The new one will struggle to match these times carrying so much extra weight. So it's just as well that Subaru UK has confirmed that a hotter 276bhp version, possibly badged STi, will come to these shores, though not until 2002.

Which is not to say the 1994cc boxer has not been improved in other respects. The addition of a close-coupled catalyst in the exhaust manifold, a tumble generating valve in the inlet and electronically controlled exhaust gas recirculation have helped it meet EU3 emissions levels, and improvements have been made to response and refinement.

The five-speed manual gearbox and all-wheel-drive system have barely changed, although revisions to the shape of the gear teeth in the 'box and final drive have reduced meshing noise, while the differential mounting points have been beefed up. Clutch effort has also been reduced by upping the diameter of the master cylinder. Torque split is 50:50 front/rear unless the viscous centre diff senses excess wheel speed at either end of the car, when it directs a higher proportion of torque to the axle with more grip. As before, a second viscous coupling between the rear wheels operates as a limited-slip differential.

SUSPENSION, STEERING, BRAKES

Retaining the low but wide flat four engine made it unlikely the new car would change from a compact strut front suspension, but there have been refinements.

Pick-up points, fixed with one eye on rally requirements, have been adjusted, as have spring and damper rates. A hydroformed front subframe is now incorporated to improve refinement, and particular attention has been paid to reducing damper friction – a bugbear of strut designs because it compromises ride quality and makes the suspension less responsive over bumpy surfaces.

ABOVE Load-carrying ability is much improved with larger boot and opening. Subaru UK insisted that rear spoiler stayed.

Subaru isn't specific about how this has been achieved, but improved seal design and increased bending stiffness are both likely candidates.

Larger changes have been made at the rear, but not the switch to a multi-link design that some predicted. Instead, struts are retained but once again fettled, with new pick-up points and revised spring and damper settings. The major alteration is to the roll-centre – the point through which cornering loads are reacted – which has been raised 33mm to bring it close to that of the WRC rally car. Subaru claims this has enhanced rear grip and reduced understeer, effects which are mutually contradictory. A raised rear roll centre normally loosens the back end, which is consistent with understeer being cut. We'll find out whether this is true or not in next week's road test.

Of the two body styles, the saloon is the one to go for if you want the ultimate in handling. As well as having a 20mm wider track it boasts a cast aluminium strut link in the front suspension to reduce unsprung mass and – principally due to its fixed rear bulkhead

THE OLD IMPREZA

Only three things needed fixing on the old Impreza Turbo: the cheapo interior, the boxer engine's thirst for unleaded, plus the tendency for the chassis to understeer when pressed. The latter was especially obvious if you took to the track, where the nose would run progressively wider as the front tyres quickly overheated.

But there was so much that was brilliant about the car that even problems as glaring as these were easy to ignore. I remember the first time I drove an Impreza Turbo, back in 1994. It was the original road test car and at the time the Impreza was a 13 grand nobody. We had no hints of what was to come.

And then, out of nowhere, came the bescooped and bewinged Impreza. I did the performance figures on that first car and I remember not being able to believe my eyes when I read the 5.8sec 0–60mph time. Even now that's fantastically quick, but back then it was off the scale for a car that cost no more than a Mondeo. And it had the brakes and handling and steering to match. Overnight it put Subaru on the map.

Since then there have been many new and improved Imprezas, versions with more power, bigger turbos, crazier performance, none more so than the hair-raising 22B. But the one I remember most affectionately is that silver saloon of 1994. The new model can't possibly be as surprising as that car, if only because it has so much to live up to.

Mind you, if Subaru really has dialled out the understeer, upgraded the interior and improved the fuel economy, it might get damn close. You'll have to read next week's road test and comparison to find out for sure.

LEFT Traditional Impreza features such as spoiler-mounted "dinner-plate" foglamps and big bonnet air scoop are present.

SPECIFICATIONS IMPREZA WRX

COST
Price	£21,495
On sale in UK	late November

HOW FAST?
0–62mph	5.9sec
Top speed	143mph

ECONOMY
Urban	19.9mpg
Extra Urban	35.8mpg
Combined	27.7mpg

DIMENSIONS
Length	4,405mm
Width	1,730mm
Height	1,440mm
Wheelbase	2,525mm
Weight	1,385kg
Fuel tank	60 litres

ENGINE
Layout	4 cyls horizontally opposed, 1,994cc
Max power	215bhp at 5,600rpm
Specific output	108bhp per litre
Power to weight	155bhp per tonne
Torque to weight	155lb ft per tonne
Installation	Front, longitudinal four-wheel drive
Bore/stroke	92/75mm
Made of	Alloy heads and block
Compression ratio	8.0:1
Valve gear	4 per cyl, dohc per bank
Ignition and fuel	Electronic ignition, multi-point fuel injection, IHI turbocharger

GEARBOX
Type 5-speed manual
Ratios/mph per 1,000rpm
Final drive 3.90
1st 3.45/5.3		2nd 1.95/9.4	
3rd 1.37/13.4		4th 0.97/18.8	
5th 0.74/24.7			

SUSPENSION
Front MacPherson strut, transverse link, coil springs, anti-roll bar
Rear MacPherson strut, trailing arm, dual link, coil springs, anti-roll bar

STEERING
Type Rack and pinion, power assisted
Turns lock-to-lock 2.75

BRAKES
Front Ventilated discs, 4-piston calipers
Rear Ventilated discs, 2-piston calipers
Anti lock Standard

WHEELS AND TYRES
Size 7.0Jx17in
Made of Cast alloy
Tyres 215/45 ZR17
Bridgestone RE011

THE **AUTOCAR** VERDICT
Sticks to the golden rule of "if it ain't broke don't fix it" on the technical front. But radical new styling makes up for that.

– superior body torsional stiffness (improved by 250 per cent over the old model, whereas the sports wagon gains by 239 per cent). Both cars now ride on larger wheels: 7xl7in rims with 215/45 ZR17 tyres.

Steering remains essentially as before – engine speed-sensitive power-assisted rack and pinion – but there have been unspecified revisions to provide improved feedback and enhance directional control at speed over bumps. A new rubber coupling within the steering universal joint and more rigid mounting of the steering rack are both said to aid refinement.

Anti-lock braking is by discs all round, as before, but Subaru reckons to have improved the weighting by adjusting the pedal leverage ratio.

SAFETY AND SECURITY
The new Impreza's weight increase is largely explained by extra body strength in the interests of crashworthiness. Particular attention has been paid to the performance in offset and multi-directional impacts. Tailored blanks – steel sheets of non-constant thickness – are used in the sill and B-post areas to up their strength while adding the minimum extra mass, and ring-shaped reinforcement frames help spread impact loads. Spin-off benefits of the bodyshell strengthening include improved refinement and, as already noted, enhanced torsional stiffness for tauter handling.

Electric pretensioners and load limiters improve the protection of front seat occupants and there is now a three-point belt for centre rear passengers.

LEFT Impreza aficionados will feel let down at the lack of a power hike; Subaru concentrated on making interior quality much higher, while head room and width have been increased.

Driver and front passenger airbags are standard; seat-fitted side airbags are also available but only in the saloon, and then only with the sports seat option. Child seat installation is improved by Isofix mountings, and a Thatcham Category 1 alarm and immobiliser are fitted as standard.

TECH VERDICT

Though it is impossible to tell without driving it, all the signs point to a more refined, grown up Impreza Turbo. One that might not be as quick against the stopwatch as before, but a more rounded car nonetheless. If Subaru's claims concerning the car's ride refinement and suspension composure are true then it won't matter so much that performance has dropped slightly. If not, the Impreza's stranglehold on the enthusiast market may suffer.

On the other hand, the new interior, vastly improved trim and superior crashworthiness are all welcome. Roll on next week's road test. Then we'll find out whether Subaru has gone in the right direction or not.

BELOW New car's profile is not radically different to predecessor's. External dimensions remain similar to old car's too.

SUBARU IMPREZA

IMPREZA WRX The hotly anticipated new Impreza WRX faces
the daunting task of replacing a stunningly effective drivers' car

Ten years ago it would have been inconceivable for a Subaru to be the most eagerly awaited performance car of the year. Not now. The new £21,495 Impreza WRX is just that car.

Since 1994 the Impreza Turbo has defined affordable performance motoring, and in the process facilitated one of the most remarkable image rethinks ever witnessed by the motor industry.

And now the Impreza has to start all over again.

You'd think that all the hard work had been done over the last seven years, but the truth is, the arrival of the new Impreza is a pivotal moment not only for the Impreza but for the company itself. In many ways it's more difficult second time around: people's expectations are far higher now.

The theme is wholly familiar: a turbocharged boxer four-cylinder engine sits longitudinally in an all-wheel-drive chassis. But this time there's a greater concession to drivetrain and chassis refinement, as well as a new name. What was the good old Turbo becomes the WRX. And Subaru UK has confirmed that in 2002 the 215bhp car will be joined by a 280bhp model, possibly badged STi.

QUICK FACTS

Model tested	Subaru Impreza WRX
List price	£21,495
Top speed	141 mph
30–70mph	5.8sec
0–60mph	5.7sec
60–0mph	2.8sec
MPG	18.7
For	Brilliant chassis and steering, refinement, value
Against	Looks, poor stereo, fuel economy

ROAD TEST

25 OCTOBER 2000

Volume 226

No 4 | 5406

WIN EDDIE JORDAN'S NSX FOR A MONTH!

AUTOCAR

FIRST UK ROAD TEST

New Impreza Turbo

Blast off! Why the best just got better

MOTOR SHOW FULL REPORT
British Motor Show 2000
Baby 1 VR shock

EXCLUSIVE TEST
Impreza vs Audi S3 vs Golf V6

X585 KOE

ROAD TEST IMPREZA WRX

MAXIMUM SPEEDS

5th 141mph/5,710rpm 4th 132/7,000
3rd 94/7,000   2nd 66/7,000
1st 37/7,000

ACCELERATION FROM REST

True mph	seconds	speedo mph
30	2.0	31
40	3.1	41
50	4.3	52
60	5.7	62
70	7.8	72
80	9.9	83
90	12.8	94
100	16.9	104

Standing qtr mile 14.5sec/95mph
Standing km 27.9sec/120mph
30–70mph through gears 5.8sec

ACCELERATION IN GEAR

MPH	5th	4th	3rd	2nd
20–40	16.3	9.6	5.6	3.2
30–50	14.5	8.0	4.3	2.6
40–60	12.2	6.4	3.6	2.6
50–70	9.6	5.3	3.6	-
60–80	8.6	5.6	3.8	-
70–90	9.4	6.0	4.6	-
80–100	10.3	6.6	-	-

BRAKES

30/50/70mph   10.3/25.3/47.2 metres
60–0mph   2.8sec

NOISE

Idle/max revs in 3rd 44/80dbA
30/50/70mph 62/69/74dbA

FUEL CONSUMPTION

Average/best/worst/touring
18.7/24.0/13.4/24.0mpg

Urban	19.9mpg
Extra urban	35.8mpg
Combined	27.7mpg
Tank capacity	60 litres
Touring range	320 miles

TESTER'S NOTES

Yet another new Bridgestone for us tyre geeks. This time it's called a Potenza RE 011 and, judging by the overall handling and ride of the Impreza, it's an absolute corker.

Why go to the expense of fitting a non-standard size hi-fi and then make it sound this limp? A head unit and speaker upgrade is what's needed. But then you've got a lovely hole in the dashboard. Not clever.

We'd like to say that there were a fair few folk who thought the Scooby rather attractive. But we'd be lying if we did. Everyone just grimaced and said: "Oh no, what have they done?" Sorry, but we agree.

It may not be anything special to look at in the daytime but at night the dash looks great. Everything has a spooky green glow to it. And in the dark you don't have to look at that silver dash surround.

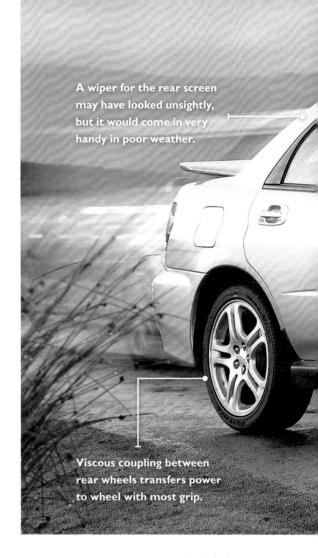

A wiper for the rear screen may have looked unsightly, but it would come in very handy in poor weather.

Viscous coupling between rear wheels transfers power to wheel with most grip.

DESIGN AND ENGINEERING ★★★★
Evolution of a proven formula

Let's deal with the main issue first: the looks. First off, rest assured that the new Impreza looks miles better in the flesh than it does in photographs. And being the WRX model it has arches with enough girth to make at least some sort of style statement.

But despite Subaru's claims that it was trying to create a shape that would improve over time and not date too quickly, the new Impreza WRX's styling is still a big disappointment. Park it next to the last of the old Turbos and the new car looks like a cruelly distorted caricature of its predecessor.

There's a lot that's carried over, though. The trademark front driving lights remain, as do the huge air intake on the bonnet and twin exhausts. The flared wheel arches are new and bear more than a passing resemblance to those found on another rally champ, the original Audi Quattro.

On balance it's a shape that's best in profile, at its weakest from the rear three-quarter and not very successful overall.

Goggle-eyed lamp units are different in Japan. They have a more complicated lens system and look even uglier.

Wheels now 17in in diameter and look more attractive. Design is almost identical to the current Legacy's alloys.

Body is 250 per cent stiffer torsionally than the old Impreza Turbo.

X585 KOE

The rest of the car still makes mouthwatering reading. At the business end sits Subaru's familiar horizontally opposed four-cylinder turbocharged engine. It retains the same 1994cc capacity and boasts the same 215bhp power output as before. Peak torque rises by just 1lb ft to 215lb ft at 3,600rpm, 400rpm lower than before.

There's no clear reason for the increase, but a new catalyst and an 11 per cent larger intercooler both make some difference. There's nothing wrong with using the same inherently excellent engine, but the power-to-weight ratio has been hit to the tune of 19bhp per tonne now that the car weighs 1,385kg according to our scales, an increase of 150kg.

The real work has gone on around the bodyshell and in fine tuning the already excellent chassis. Torsional rigidity was the main goal and Subaru has achieved a whopping 250 per cent increase over the old car in saloon form. That leaves a much more solid platform on which the all-round MacPherson strut suspension can do its stuff. New pick-up points for the suspension, a redesigned front subframe, revised spring and damper ratings and a 33mm rise

LEFT Engine given only minor changes.

LEFT High lip lets down usefully big boot.

ABOVE Roomier cabin falls short of German quality, and wheel still lacks reach adjustment. Driving position is excellent.

Given maximum revs and a side-stepped clutch, the new WRX catapults itself from 0–30mph in just 2.0sec. One extremely swift gearchange later and 60mph arrives in just 5.7sec. Sustain the tempo and 100mph whizzes by in 16.9sec, the standing quarter mile in 14.5sec. Top speed at a rather blustery high-speed bowl was 141mph.

In isolation that's a very impressive set of figures, one that would take 231bhp of BMW 330i to beat. But there are a couple of snags. First, the figures show it to be considerably slower than the old car against the clock (that managed 5.3sec to 60mph and 14.9sec to 100mph, and did 143mph flat out). Second, the subjective impressions support such numerical shortfalls.

No matter what gear you're in or what speed you're travelling at, the Impreza no longer hurls you up the road in the brutal manner we've come to expect. Throttle response is good rather than exceptional for a turbo motor, with boost coming in as low as 2,500rpm. But the mid-range isn't as strong as before and even though the rev limiter is set at 7,400rpm, anything beyond 6,500rpm and the performance starts to tail away.

Again, the in-gear times are impressive in isolation but well down on before. In fifth gear it manages the 50–70mph drag in 9.6sec, up from 8.5sec. And from 30–50mph in fourth it needs 8.0sec, a disappointing 2.0sec slower than before.

But that's where the bad news stops. This Impreza strikes a brilliant balance between refinement and character and makes you wonder why anyone bothers making in-line fours when they're so much rougher than the Impreza's boxer. It may not be as fast as the old car, but with the extra refinement it's almost as satisfying.

The gearshift and clutch are markedly improved too. There's less resistance and still a short, snappy throw.

Brakes have long been an Impreza strong point, and these maintain that tradition. Pedal feel is better than before; they didn't fade once, and they gave every driver real confidence.

in the overall roll centre of the car should make quite a difference to the driving experience. The focus was on extra refinement and added adjustability, according to Subaru.

Tyre and wheel diameters rise to 17in, with 215/45 tyres all round. The wheels are an open-spoke design and leave a clear view of the ventilated discs (294mm front, 266mm rear) fitted as standard. There's no traction control, just a limited-slip differential at the back.

Big changes have been made to the interior, the one area where the old car attracted real criticism. An all-new dashboard and centre console houses nothing more imaginative than the usual stereo and rotary heater controls. It's difficult not to think that rather more than this was needed to tempt people away from more stylish European rivals.

PERFORMANCE/BRAKES ★★★★
More refinement, better gearbox, less pace

What a relief. Subaru may be trying to add some deportment to the Impreza's CV by making it quieter and more refined, but it still had the foresight to make the WRX get off the line with plenty of drama.

HANDLING AND RIDE ★★★★★
A near faultless performance

Where do you start with a car whose overall ability might just rewrite the manual on performance saloon handling? With the bits that are different.

Subaru seems to have taken the concept of comfort to heart, because in a stroke it has turned the Impreza from being something to avoid over long distances into a comfortable saloon. New spring and damper ratings all round have given the suspension a compliance totally at odds with its ability to keep body movements under check at ridiculously high speeds. No matter what the surface, the car just copes.

So the Scooby's gone soft in its old age? Not likely. Subaru is now so adept at making four-wheel-drive cars handle neutrally – and in the new Impreza's case throttle-adjustable as well – that it's difficult to tell which wheels are actually doing the driving.

As before, traction out of any bend is superb. But put the power down mid-corner and the car just tightens its line and scoots off looking for the next bend. Back off in the same situation and the line tightens immediately. There's almost no understeer. And this hasn't come at the expense of a twitchy rear end either. Grip is stunning wet or dry, but a large lift will unstick the back tyres, courtesy of the raised rear roll centre.

And the biggest treat is still to come. This car's steering is quite brilliant, although it takes some time to get used to it. At first it feels too light and not quite sharp enough: under-sensitive even. Nor is it a particularly quick rack at 2.8 turns lock to lock. There's

not that much resistance off the straight-ahead either, and in corners it doesn't load up very much.

But with time you learn to appreciate such subtleties and realise that this is one of the few systems that can play a sporting and cruising role equally well. Delicacy and accuracy are its two best traits. Combined with such a deeply talented chassis, it provides you with total confidence in the front end of the car and refuses to kick back even on

BELOW Acceleration and top speed suffer in comparison with the outgoing Impreza Turbo, but the new WRX is the better all-round high-performance package.

WHAT IT COSTS

SUBARU IMPREZA WRX

On-the-road price	£21,495
Price as tested	£21,495

INSURANCE

Insurance/typical quote	17/£942

WARRANTY

36 months/60,000 miles, 6 years rust

SERVICING

Major 15,000 miles Minor 7,500 miles

EQUIPMENT CHECKLIST

Air conditioning	■
Traction control	-
Leather trim	-
Reach/rake-adjust steering column	-/■
Anti-lock brakes	■
Airbag driver/passenger	■/■
Satellite navigation	-
Alarm/immobiliser	■/■
RDS stereo/CD player	■/■

■ = Standard na = not available

SPECIFICATIONS IMPREZA WRX

DIMENSIONS

Min/max front leg room 920/1,120mm Min/max rear leg room 640/850mm
Min/max front head room 920/1,110mm Interior width front/rear 1,430/1,430mm
Boot length 970mm Boot height 380mm Min/max boot width 960/1,340mm
VDA boot volume na Front/rear tracks 1,485/1,480mm Kerb weight 1,385kg
Weight distribution front/rear 60/40 Width 1,730mm inc mirrors

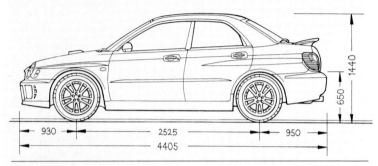

ENGINE

Layout	4 cyls horizontally opposed, 1,994cc
Max power	215bhp at 5,600rpm
Max torque	215lb ft at 3,600rpm
Specific output	108bhp per litre
Power to weight	155bhp per tonne
Torque to weight	155lb ft per tonne
Installation	Front, longitudinal, four-wheel drive
Construction	Alloy heads and block
Bore/stroke	92.0/75.0mm
Valve gear	4 valves per cylinder, dohc per bank
Compression	ratio 8.0:1
Ignition and fuel	Electronic ignition, sequential fuel injection, IHI turbocharger with intercooler

TRANSMISSION

Gearbox 5-speed manual
Ratios/mph per 1,000rpm
Final drive 3.90

1st	3.45/5.3	2nd	1.95/9.4
3rd	1.37/13.4	4th	0.97/18.8
5th	0.74/24.7		

CHASSIS AND BODY

Body	5-door Saloon
Wheels	7x17in
Made of	Alloy
Tyres	215/45 ZR17 Bridgestone Potenza RE 011
Spare	Space saver

STEERING

Type Rack and pinion, power assisted
Turns lock-to-lock 2.8
Turning circle 11.0m

SUSPENSION

Front MacPherson struts, transverse link, coil springs, anti-roll bar
Rear MacPherson struts, trailing arm, dual link, coil springs, anti-roll bar

BRAKES

Front 294mm ventilated discs
Rear 266mm ventilated discs
Anti-lock Standard

the worst mid-corner bumps. And all Subaru did was modify the universal joint within the rack and mount it more rigidly. Extraordinary.

SAFETY AND EQUIPMENT ★★★★
Practical and safe but still too bland

The Impreza WRX is a big improvement over the outgoing car inside, but it's still no Audi or BMW.

Subtle new curves shape a new dash and centre console arrangement that looks distinctly Japanese without being typically Subaru. The silver spray can has been put to work on the plastic surrounding the instruments and the hi-fi. It brings some relief to an otherwise dark space, though the cabin still looks plain compared with those of its more polished German rivals.

The instruments themselves aren't particularly attractive, but they're well placed and very visible. The driving position is spot-on, despite the fact that the steering wheel adjusts for rake only. The seats are typical Impreza: supportive and comfortable in equal measure, now height-adjustable too.

Cabin space is much better than before. There's 21mm extra width front and rear and a sizeable 30mm extra head room too. It may not be quite as roomy as a Ford Mondeo, but Subaru can rightly call the WRX a five-seater. The boot's a good size too, although the load height is taller than average.

Standard equipment is generous, but as ever with Subaru the list of options is short. As standard you get electric windows all round, CD player, air conditioning and those 17in alloys. But fancy interior materials, satellite navigation and a sunroof are all missing from the options list. The quality of the stereo is also far worse than in most rivals.

Safety standards are impressive. To start with there's the new bodyshell, which features more robust side impact bars and reinforced B-pillars and seat mounting points. Twin airbags at the front are standard, but side bags will cost extra and are only available with the optional sports seats (not fitted to the test car).

ECONOMY ★★
Simply too thirsty

Shares in oil companies are rising, and they're set to rise further if the Impreza sells. Even if you refrain from using too many revs, fuel consumption remains a concern. We couldn't better 24.0mpg on our

Almost the old car's performance, but now more refined. Great value, too.

economy route, and charging across country this fell to a measly 13.4mpg. Worst of all, over the week-long period we drove the car it averaged only 18.7mpg, providing a disappointing real-world range of less than 250 miles from the 60-litre tank.

MARKET & FINANCE ★★★★
Only doubt is effect of looks on resale values

Looks could play a decisive role in the Impreza's fortunes. We're already hearing reports of customers cancelling orders because they can't get on with the shape. Nevertheless the order books are bulging.

There's nothing else to stand between the WRX and another display of residual values that will have rival manufacturers green with envy, assuming the car is as bulletproof as it was before. Subaru will restrict supply, so there will not be a glut of used cars, and there's no reason to expect anything other than a top performance from the dealers. It still comes with a full three-year/60,000-mile warranty.

AUTOCAR VERDICT

It takes time to appreciate the new Impreza WRX's full range of qualities. At face value it appears to offer less than before. Less performance, less style. But the more miles we did in it, the more we realised Subaru has achieved just what it wanted, and has in the process built something even more special.

The key to its appeal is its drivetrain and chassis refinement. It is now an extremely comfortable long-distance machine. But it also offers an incredible depth of dynamic ability. It can't help but be a more satisfying ownership proposition.

No, it doesn't blow your socks off in a straight line like before, and yes it still drinks fuel at a worrying rate. But sample it over some choice A and B roads a few times, and then on a motorway, and you'll soon realise just how brilliant it is as a package.

And at £21,495 it's far cheaper than its German rivals, most of which aren't close to matching it as a driver's car.

If you can live with the looks, the WRX remains the definitive affordable performance saloon for the enthusiast.

Styling aside, a stunning achievement   ★★★★★

STi OF THE STORM

IMPREZA WRX STi With scorching performance and awesome traction, is the new STi the best Impreza ever?

Official, the 280bhp, 155mph Subaru Impreza STi you see here does not exist yet – at least not in the UK. Subaru's official importer wants to make us wait 18 months or more before we can buy one here.

Which is a great pity because, having just spent the day howling around the Cotswolds in one, I can tell you: it's one hell of a car.

No matter. If you can't wait until 2002 to get your hands on one (and if you like this sort of car, I strongly suggest you don't wait), there is an alternative.

Step one, make sure you have £31,995 in your bank account. Step two, get a map and find Malmesbury on the map (it's in Wiltshire, about 10 miles south of Cirencester, just off the M4). Step three, get yourself along to David Hendry Sports Cars (tel 01666 824369) and ask them nicely if you can have a go in one of their demonstrator STis. Step four, get ready to make one of the easiest purchasing decisions of your life.

Why? Because if you're into this type of car you will, I guarantee, not be able to resist writing out a cheque there and then. So make sure you tell the missus where you're going before you set off.

Ah, but surely you don't get a warranty if you buy through a grey importer like Hendry, I hear you say. And the speedo probably reads in kilometres per hour while the radio tries to pick up Hiroshima FM.

Nope. Hendry will make all the alterations for you and throw in a three-year warranty and Thatcham category one alarm. Which means what you're

QUICK FACTS

Model	Subaru Impreza WRX STi
Price	£31,995
On sale in UK	Now
0–60mph	4.6sec (est)
0–100mph	11.0sec (est)
Top speed	155mph (est)

NEW CARS

14 FEBRUARY 2001

Volume 227

No 7 | 5421

AUTOCAR
Exclusive
Best ever
Impreza

Hot STi vs new Evo
First taste of showdown the world's waiting for
Plus New Peugeot 307 ● BMW M3 road test ● Shock new Aston

X861 NAM

David Hendry Performance Cars Tel. 01666 824369

STi
SUBARU TECNICA
INTERNATIONAL

ABOVE Dashboard gains chrome-rimmed dials and keeps hardcore sporting details like the switch for the intercooler water spray. Every inch says this car means business.

OPPOSITE Myriad styling tweaks differentiate STi from regular WRX; bigger STi-badged intercooler helps 2.0-litre boxer engine unleash up to 310bhp; suspension struts are unique to STi; in-your-face styling includes gold alloys.

looking at is a rather delicious piece of motoring future, right here and now, courtesy of some quick and clever thinking on the part of the Hendry family.

If you're somehow not familiar with the Impreza Turbo story, it goes a bit like this. For many years there was a company called Subaru, which produced weird and not very wonderful machines that few people cared about, cars like the XT coupé and the Justy.

Then came the Impreza, since when Subaru has been regarded as a kind of thinking man's alternative to BMW with four-wheel drive and a slice of left-foot braking thrown in for free.

Well, just as BMW has its M division to turn humble Threes and Fives into hot rods, so Subaru has STi – Subaru Technica International. And when the STi guys gets their teeth into something, the results are usually spectacular – and never more so than here.

Outwardly there are myriad styling tweaks that

differentiate the STi Impreza from the regular WRX, and they create a much more dramatic effect in the metal. The sills are colour coded, the air intake on the bonnet is bigger, the wheels are gold and only partially conceal huge great Brembo brake calipers which are also sprayed gold.

The rear windows on this particular example are also blacked out, though officially that's not legal in the UK so the factory cars won't be equipped with these. Pity this, because although it sounds tarty, the Marmite glass lends the car a lot of extra presence on the road.

Specification wise, the STi Scooby is a technophile's dream come true. Lift the bonnet and you're greeted by the most amazing sight of hundreds of different coloured leads and hoses all beautifully integrated in and around the 1994cc turbocharged boxer engine. There's also a huge air-cooler with STi inscribed in among the fins in bright red ink.

Subaru claims as much as 80 per cent of this

'NOTHING CAN PREPARE YOU FOR WHAT THIS CAR IS CAPABLE OF ON A WET AND WINDY B-ROAD'

engine is new, but the bits that count are the new variable valve timing system, the bigger air-to-air intercooler and the forged pistons that help it rev beyond 8,000rpm. Power is officially quoted at 280bhp, but only because that's the limit imposed by the Japanese legislators. In reality Hendry reckons it has about 310bhp at 6,400rpm, as well as a lot more torque than the old STi VI engine, the official figure being 275lb ft at 4,000rpm.

On their own, these improvements would be enough to ensure the STi had blistering performance compared to the previous-generation WRX, despite putting on a few extra kilos largely in the name of safety. But when mated to a new close-ratio six-speed gearbox they're said to make even more of a difference. Lag, by all accounts, is now virtually nonexistent on the road – a claim that, on paper, is hard to believe.

The chassis is fundamentally the same as the ordinary WRX's with one or two STi bits thrown in for good measure. There's a slightly quicker steering rack, uprated bushes and beefier suspension arms front and rear, and bigger Brembo brakes. But the most significant difference is the fitment of a limited-slip differential at the front, to match the one at the back; a vital piece of kit denied drivers of the regular WRX. This isn't fitted to all STis: in Japan the car comes in three trim levels ranging from KL (no front diff), via EL (front diff but no gas discharge headlights or blacked-out rear windows) to GL, which gets the full complement of hardcore hairiness. It's almost certain that a bastardised version of the GL is what we'll get in 2002. And naturally it's a GL that Hendry has let us loose in.

Snuggling down into the high sided and rather smart looking STi-logoed seat, it's obvious how much plusher the cabin is compared to the regular Impreza WRX. Slivers of alloy-look plastic surround the gearlever, stereo and heater controls, and the instruments are chrome-rimmed too. There's even a button to adjust the point at which the change-up buzzer sounds, while the water spray switches of the previous STi VI are thankfully still present. While being able to blow a fine spray of water across the face of the intercooler may not be the most vital piece of standard equipment to make use of on your way down to Tesco's, it's all part of Subaru's way of preparing you for what's to come.

Except, of course, nothing can prepare you for what this car is capable of on a wet and windy B-road. Not even a Mitsubishi Evo VI. Yep, you read that

SPECIFICATIONS WRX STi

ECONOMY

Best/worst	24.4/14.9mpg

DIMENSIONS

Length	4,405mm
Width	1,990mm
Height	1,440mm
Wheelbase	2,525mm
Weight	1,400kg
Fuel tank	60 litres

ENGINE

Layout	4 cyls horizontally opposed, 1,994cc
Max power	280bhp at 6,400rpm
Max torque	275lb ft at 4,000rpm
Specific output	140bhp per litre
Power to weight	200bhp per tonne
Torque to weight	196lb ft per tonne
Installation	Front, longitudinal
Bore/stroke	92.0/75.0mm
Made of	Cast alloy heads and block
Compression ratio	8.0:1
Valve gear	4 per cyl, dohc per bank
Ignition and fuel	STi electronic ignition, IHI turbocharger, intercooler

All figures are manufacturer's claims,
except those relating to performance

GEARBOX

Type 6-speed manual by STi
Ratios/mph per 1,000rpm
Final drive 3.90

1st	3.64/5.2	2nd	2.37/8.0
3rd	1.76/10.8	4th	1.35/14.1
5th	1.06/18.0	6th	0.84/22.7

SUSPENSION

Front MacPherson struts, coil springs, anti-roll bar
Rear MacPherson struts, coil springs, trailing arms, anti-roll bar

STEERING

Type Rack and pinion, power assisted
Turns lock-to-lock 2.7

BRAKES

Front 294mm ventilated discs
Rear 266mm ventilated discs
Anti lock Standard

WHEELS AND TYRES

Size 7.0Jx17in
Made of Cast alloy
Tyres 225/45 ZR17 Bridgestone RE040

THE **AUTOCAR** VERDICT

The definitive evolution of a definitive car. The Evo VII will have to be truly special to win the crown back for Mitsubishi.

Straight-line performance is awesome. But what's even more impressive is the excellence of the STi's steering – especially as the ride is better than the Evo VI's.

correctly: the STi is at last the car that puts the Evo in its place. And I know this from experience, having put the two back to back for the day. Although judging from our first drive of the Evo VII it may not stay that way for long.

To begin with, the only aspects that appear notably different from the regular WRX are the firmer ride (it's hard but not crashy), the slightly heavier and quicker steering, the meatier brakes and the super-short throw gearchange. But the first time you put your foot down and hold it there for more than a second, one very big difference hits you: unlike the regular WRX, the STi goes. Really goes. Just guessing, I'd say it'd do 60mph somewhere in the mid fours or 100mph in 10–11sec. So in other words it's as quick as, if not quicker than, an Evo.

Subaru's claims that the STi has less lag are true up to a point but there's still a delay between opening the throttle and the meat of the acceleration actually starting – about a second by my reckoning. But once the mayhem starts it just keeps on coming, and all you do is pick off another gear before the 8,100rpm limiter intrudes to sustain the outrageous momentum.

Get the STi moving above 50mph on A and B-roads and fourth, fifth and sixth are the only gears you need to use. Third is just a toy to bring out on special occasions while second is purely for showing off.

Yet what makes the STi so eye-wateringly capable across country, and so unique among its peers, is not its engine or its straight-line performance. It's the chassis, and more specifically its steering precision and basic suspension control. Thanks to all the electronic trickery contained within the various diffs front and rear it always has massive traction, wet or dry.

But unlike the Evo it also has an uncanny ability to soak up intrusions and simply glide over rough ground seemingly unhindered by scars and ruts. It also suffers from a lot less steering fidget than an Evo and is simply more composed for more of the time over rough surfaces, which is an absolutely crucial element considering the state of most of our roads.

No, it's maybe not as raw-knuckle exciting over a 10 minute balls-out blast. But once the red mist fades and you're left with the realities of everyday motoring, it's convincingly the better car. I think I'd even rate it above the forthcoming new M3 in most respects, simply because you can use more of its performance

without attracting so much attention to yourself while doing so. In an era of cameras and anti-speed campaigning, such qualities are increasingly relevant.

The only question mark over the Impreza STi is when and where to buy one. Either you can wait two years for the official versions to filter through to Britain, or you can order one now via an outfit like Hendry. Doesn't sound like much of a dilemma to me.

BELOW STi's interior feels much plusher than regular Impreza WRX, with alloy-effect plastics and blue cloth; new sports seats are comfortable, supportive and stylish.

MODS SET THE TREND

IMPREZA WRX UK300 The new Impreza WRX UK300 offers styling and tuning options, courtesy of Prodrive, to make your WRX stand out from the crowd

First things first. This Impreza may have been fettled by Prodrive and it may have a body kit styled by Peter Stevens but it's no hot P1. Not by a long shot.

This is the Subaru Impreza WRX UK300. It's the first of what is likely to be a long list of uprated WRXs, created to satisfy our hunger for ever-faster Imprezas.

As its name suggests, the UK300 is aimed at Subaru fans in Britain and only 300 will be built. Well, perhaps 'built' is not quite the right word. Styled and chipped is a better way of describing its transition from standard blown Scooby to UK300.

It's a two-step process that's available on any standard WRX once it has been registered. No need for type-approval then. The styling kit, a £3500 option, injects the rather gawky-looking WRX with a real spurt of rally-style menace. A fair proportion of that money goes on bigger 18in gold OZ alloys shod with aggressive 225/40 Pirelli P-Zero Rosso tyres. Then there are those headlamp units – a trio of individually mounted dipped, full-beam and indicator lenses set in high gloss plastic that gives the WRX a space alien visage.

The final touch is a pair of aerodynamic aids. You can hardly miss the ugly Prodrive-badged rear wing. Mounted on two struts high above the bootlip the aerofoil looks like an electricity pylon has got a touch too intimate with the car's rear end. The front end gets a subtle black bib below the standard foglamps and Subaru claims both additions reduce lift at speed.

QUICK FACTS

Model	Subaru Impreza WRX UK300
Price	£26,595
On sale in UK	Now
0–60mph	5.2sec (est)
Top speed	150mph (est)

SPECIFICATIONS WRX UK300

ECONOMY
Urban	17.5mpg (est)
Extra urban	28.8mpg (est)
Combined	25.2mpg(est)
CO_2 emissions	270g/km (est)

DIMENSIONS
Length	4,405mm
Width	1,730mm
Height	1,440mm
Wheelbase	2,525mm
Weight	1,385kg
Fuel tank	60 litres

ENGINE
Layout	4 cyls horizontally opposed, 1,994cc
Max power	240bhp at 6,500rpm
Max torque	261lb ft at 4,000rpm
Specific output	120bhp per litre
Power to weight	173bhp per tonne
Installation	Front, longitudinal, four-wheel drive
Bore/stroke	92.0/75.0mm
Made of	Alloy heads and block
Compression ratio	8.0:1
Valve gear	4 per cylinder, dohc
Ignition and fuel	Electronic ignition, sequential multi-point injection, IHI turbocharger with intercooler

All figures are manufacturer's claims

GEARBOX
Type 5-speed manual
Ratios/mph per 1,000rpm
Final drive 3.90

1st 3.45/5.5		2nd 1.95/9.8	
3rd 1.37/13.9		4th 0.97/19.7	
5th 0.74/25.8			

SUSPENSION
Front MacPherson struts, transverse link, coil springs, anti-roll bar
Rear MacPherson struts, trailing arm, dual link, coil springs, anti-roll bar

STEERING
Type Rack and pinion, power assisted
Turns lock-to-lock 2.8

BRAKES
Front 294mm ventilated discs
Rear 266mm ventilated discs
Anti lock Standard

WHEELS AND TYRES
Size 7.5Jx18
Made of Alloy
Tyres 225/40 ZR18 Pirelli P-Zero Rosso

THE **AUTOCAR** VERDICT
First of many expected hot Impreza WRXs. A stopgap until the manic STi arrives but expensive and not particularly quick.

To identify the car as a limited edition, there are a handful of rather brash UK300 badges stuck to the bodywork. The interior remains virtually unchanged, bar blue Alcantara inserts on the grippy Recaro chairs and another UK300 sticker mounted above the rear view mirror. No tasteful Alpina-style aluminium strip to announce the car's production number here.

You'll need another £1,600 for the performance upgrade to give the WRX some bite to match its bark. But rather than revert to traditional power extraction methods like boring and stroking, boosting pressure or installing hotter cams, Prodrive has simply reprogrammed the engine management system, pulled out one of the three catalytic converters and replaced the twin exhaust pipe with a single bazooka-style tube.

It may not sound mechanically exciting but the hotter chip works. Power from the flat-four steps up from 215bhp to 240bhp at 5,600rpm and torque climbs by 46lb ft to 261lb ft at 4,000rpm, 600rpm higher than before.

That's the extent of the mechanical changes, so you're left with standard WRX hardware. That means MacPherson struts front and rear, five-speed manual gearbox, rack-and-pinion steering, ventilated brake

discs behind each wheel, that bullet-proof all-wheel-drive system, and probably one of the most talented chassis in the business.

The UK300 is quick, but not blindingly so. Although Subaru quotes no official figures, a chat with its engineers turns up some roughly estimated times: they reckon the standstill to 60mph scamper should take just over five seconds and the WRX should touch 150mph. Which makes it just a fraction faster than the original Impreza Turbo or a well run-in WRX – a little disappointing if you're a new Impreza owner looking to instill some of the hard-edged performance that made the old Subaru such a stormer. And even more frustrating for those buyers waiting for a replacement for the storming Impreza P1. They will have to bite their nails while waiting for the official arrival of the wildcat STi.

It's the UK300's increase in torque that makes itself more noticeable than the power upgrade. At standstill the engine idles with a lumpier, grumpier exhaust note. Work through the gears and the flat four motor feels robust and deep-lunged, spinning effortlessly to its 7,500rpm limiter with less of the high-rev breathlessness that afflicts the standard WRX. That big bore exhaust emits a stunning noise

as you accelerate hard – there's a whistling blast of air like Louis Armstrong blowing very hard through a straw to counter the engine's off-beat rhythm.

And that wider spread of torque also helps mask off-boost torpor – you just need to flex your right foot in the taller gears to dispatch slower traffic rather than drop down a gear.

The rest, being an Impreza, verges on the sublime. The ride is still fabulously damped despite the bigger alloys and more aggressive tyres. The car flies through bends with an unflustered stance, cornering flatly. The scalpel-sharp steering is delightfully accurate and creates a vital link between Pirellis and palms. The gearlever shifts with a honed feel and the brakes dispense with speed as quickly as the engine piles it on.

Our advice? Go for the engine upgrade and stash your £3,500 for that cosmetic pack in the bank. You'll add a bit of Q-car status to your Scooby while your financial prudence will pay off when the STi arrives and you find it impossible to resist.

So, the proliferation of WRX's has begun. While the UK300 has neither the looks nor the heart rate, it signposts the way for future hotter Imprezas. And that's no bad thing.

ABOVE Performance upgrade provides 240bhp, 25bhp up on standard WRX.

OPPOSITE New rally-style headlamps and 18in gold OZ alloys included in £3,500 styling kit.

SCOOBY'S STi

Until now, the only way to lay hands on an Impreza STi was via the grey import route, but Subaru's latest WRC-bred bruiser will soon be officially on sale in the UK

Talk about déjà vu – despite this being the official launch of the keenly anticipated Subaru Impreza STi, I've already driven an STi three times this year. All were imported from Japan but unlike today's car, none by Subaru UK. So this, finally, is The Real Thing.

And that's both good news and bad. The good? Subaru has adopted an aggressive pricing policy – the standard STi will cost £25,995 when it goes on sale next January, while the Prodrive-enhanced version driven here will still cost only £27,495. That's some way short of the 30 grand importers have been charging for grey STis since the beginning of this year, and a lot less than the expected £30k Colt Cars UK is likely to charge for an official Mitsubishi Evo VII next year.

And the bad? The STi produces only 262bhp, some 18bhp less than Japanese domestic models. Blame strict Euro IV emissions regulations and our lower octane rated fuel for the power cut.

It's still an ugly thing, but the STi finally gets a decent dose of visual aggression. A new bespoke grille sits above a gaping front air intake, and there are sinister black-backed headlamps and a bigger bonnet mounted air intake. The visual tweaks are topped off by deeper body-coloured side sills. Factor in 17in gold alloys and a more assertive body kit, and the STi looks so much meaner.

Pop the aluminium bonnet and you're faced with the tentacled manifold of the Scooby's flat four topped by an imposing STi-logoed intercooler. But this is not a mildly fettled WRX engine – up to 80 per cent of the componentry is new. The all-alloy boxer engine

QUICK FACTS

Model	Subaru Impreza STi Prodrive
Price	£27,495
On sale in UK	January
0–60mph	5.2sec
Top speed	148mph

NEW CARS

12 DECEMBER 2001

Volume 230

No 11 | 5464

AUTOCAR
Every Wednesday

EXCLUSIVE FIRST DRIVE
Beautiful, beastly new
LOTUS ESPRIT

SCOOP!
We unmask Porsche's
secret McLaren-beater

BELOW Prodrive interior classy; wrong-slotting close-gated gearshift is easy.

gets variable inlet-valve timing and a bigger IHI turbo and intercooler. The result: 262bhp at 6,000rpm and 253lb ft at 4,000rpm.

Opt for the Prodrive version, as Subaru expects most buyers will, and you get a further-modified grille, even meaner front bumper and an enormous rear spoiler.

A six-speed STi gearbox is new, too. It transfers power to a viscous coupling that juggles torque between the front and rear ends according to grip levels. And both axles are now fitted with limited-slip diffs for the best possible traction. The rack-and-pinion steering has more aggressive gearing: just 2.6 turns between locks.

There's more stopping power, too. The thumping great 330mm ventilated front discs are gripped by four-pot aluminium calipers while 305mm discs with two-pot calipers work the rear end. The mechanical upgrade is completed by a thoroughly revised suspension package: the struts at the back are now inverted, WRC style, to provide more travel and great strength and are fitted with uprated springs and dampers while the wheels grow to 17in and wear 225/45 ZR17 Bridgestones.

Drop into the cosseting Recaro seat, adjust the Momo steering wheel and it's easy to find a good driving position. You sit lower than you do in an Evo VII, too, and immediately feel part of the car.

At idle the single big-bore exhaust coughs out a gruffer version of the offbeat warble unique to Subaru flat fours. Snick the tallish gearlever into first gear – it needs a firm shove – ease the progressive clutch out, feed in the throttle smartly, and you can't help feeling, well, just a bit disappointed. Why? Because even by 2,500rpm under full throttle the turbo is still yawning. For the full effect you need at least 3,500rpm before there's any real action, which is one thing that immediately distances this car from the Evo.

Get caught below that threshold and you might as well be driving a standard WRX. But by the time the engine hits 4,000rpm, its low-rev lethargy is forgotten. Then the turbocharger lights up the engine like an

afterburner and from there to the 7,000rpm red line delivers dramatic thrust accompanied by a worthy WRC-style soundtrack. It almost feels cammy and Subaru's figures of 5.2sec to 60mph and 148mph top speed actually seem slightly pessimistic. The engine is wonderfully smooth and refined as well.

Six gears help extract the performance effectively as well. The well-chosen ratios ensure that, taken to the red line in each gear, the engine stays well inside the power zone with every upshift.

The harder you drive, the harder the STi responds. Body control is just about flawless, the chassis never feels less than composed no matter how fast or aggressively you drive, and grip levels are outstanding. The all-wheel-drive hardware has also been set up to allow you to dial out understeer and slingshot neutrally out of corners if you're brave enough to keep the throttle planted all the way round.

The brakes deserve special praise, too – they shed huge chunks of speed with a calmness that matches the chassis' nonchalance. The pedals are well placed for heel and toeing, and working the gearbox is the sort of indulgence you'll find yourself warming to just to hear that charismatic flat-four bark and grumble up and down the rev range.

But if the STi's handling impresses, then its ride quality simply astounds. It's superbly compliant and damped considering how much control there is at high speed. The suspension sponges away intrusions – an extraordinary achievement for such a focused driving weapon. Yet, despite this softer than expected set-up, there's no a trace of wallow or lurch. Evo VII drivers would be fibbing if they claimed as much.

At motorway speeds, that serene ride quality combined with the silken boxer engine means the STi feels more like a comfortable GT than a rally-bred blaster. The intelligent gearing helps here, too – at 80mph the engine is on the right side of 3,500rpm, so slower traffic and inclines are dispatched with the smallest throttle tweaks. It could also mean you'll see the other side of 30mpg on motorway runs.

In many ways the STi is actually a more rounded car than the Evo VII. Some of the lairiness of the previous grey import STi models has gone, replaced by a new found finesse. But the best news is that it now exists in an official capacity in the UK. At last Subaru UK has seen the light and given us a proper STi Impreza to play with, and although it may not be as thrilling as an Evo in absolute terms, that isn't really the point. Especially as the Subaru is so well priced. For enthusiasts everywhere, the STi is extremely welcome.

SPECIFICATIONS STi PRODRIVE

ECONOMY

Urban	16.9mpg
Extra urban	29.7mpg
Combined	23.3mpg
CO$_2$ emissions	290g/km

DIMENSIONS

Length	4,405mm
Width	1,730mm
Height	1,440mm
Wheelbase	2,525mm
Weight	1,470kg
Fuel tank	60 litres

ENGINE

Layout	4 cyls horizontally opposed, 1,994cc
Max power	262bhp at 6,000rpm
Max torque	253lb ft at 4,000rpm
Power to weight	178lb ft per tonne
Power to weight	178lb ft per tonne
Power to torque	172lb ft per tonne
Installation	Front, longitudinal, four-wheel drive
Bore/stroke	92/75mm
Made of	Alloy head and block
Compression ratio	8.0:1
Valve gear	4 valves per cylinder, dohc
Ignition and fuel	Electronic ignition, multi-point fuel injection, IHI turbocharger

GEARBOX

Type 6-speed manual
Ratios/mph per 1,000rpm
Final drive 3.9

1st	3.64/5.2	2nd	2.37/8.0
3rd	1.76/10.8	4th	1.35/14.1
5th	1.06/18.0	6th	0.84/22.7

SUSPENSION

Front and rear MacPherson struts, coil springs, anti-roll bar

STEERING

Type Rack and pinion, power-assisted
Turns lock-to-lock 2.6

BRAKES

Front 330mm ventilated discs
Rear 305mm ventilated discs
Anti lock Standard with EBD

WHEELS AND TYRES

Size 7.0J x 17in
Made of Cast alloy
Tyres Bridgestone Potenza RE040 225/45 ZR 17

THE AUTOCAR VERDICT

STi at last adds ballistic performance to the Impreza's official UK vocabulary. A formidable, easy-to-live-with all-rounder

All figures are manufacturer's claims

PUNCH AT A PRICE

IMPREZA WRX Final report: We love the WRX. We even like the WRX's dealer. It's just that we've seen too much of him. *By Phil McNamara*

It was late August when I spotted the immaculate Y-plate Subaru Impreza WRX on the garage's forecourt as I dropped my own WRX off for yet another service. The 7,200-miler's sticker price was £18,995 – £2,500 less than new – and a tantalising price for such a performance icon.

But why was such a new and desirable machine for sale so soon? "The owner loved it but couldn't afford to run it," said the dealer. That owner's tenure lasted only five months; I ran *Autocar*'s WRX for 10 months. And now that it's no longer with us, do I agree with his epitaph?

No doubt about it, the WRX (or Rex as it swiftly became known) was one of the most popular cars on our fleet in 2001. Too popular for my liking, ensuring Rex was hardly a faithful companion. In its first two months in my charge, I spent just two weekends with it. The editor proved particularly fond of pulling rank, while the road testers often found vital cross-country trips for the Impreza to undertake.

Not until late January, and my first extended road trip, was I formally introduced to a WRX speciality: its chassis is more clingy than a toddler on his first walk to school.

My mission was a weekend blast from Enfield to Brighton and back, in such relentless rain that it almost made a jet-ski preferable. The Impreza handled the sodden M25 and A23 with aplomb, with not even momentary loss of traction despite deep surface water. Few chassis offer such reassurance, and the experience set me up for 20,000-plus miles of supremely confident motoring.

Many were racked up on the M25, thanks to my 120-mile daily commute. Rex proved an adept motorway-muncher, noticeably more refined than its Impreza Turbo predecessor. At m-way speeds, engine

noise was imperceptible, wind noise minimal, and the ride superb. Road test ed Chris Harris described the WRX as the best-damped tool on the sensible side of a Porsche 911.

Only excessive tyre noise punctured the tranquillity, and that was my fault: I changed the standard Bridgestone Potenza 215/45 ZR17s for Michelin Pilot Sports. The Bridgestones had lasted 11,300 miles, pretty much average wear for a turbocharged Impreza, according to our dealer, Marlborough West London. They quoted £160 a tyre, Kwik-Fit £179.95 or £700 for a set. Micheldever Tyres (01962 774437) quoted £462.68 for the standard Bridgestones, but clinched my business with £490 for the Michelins, including balancing and alignment.

That wasn't the only price I paid, however. Tyre roar became intrusive, and the Michelins proved less adept at ironing out undulations. Durability improved, however: at 25,600 miles, there was still 5mm of rubber left all round.

Although the decibels increased, the thrills did not diminish. Care to share my favourite Impreza traits? First, the moment the rev counter hits 3,500rpm, the turbocharger takes hold and the acceleration catapults the car forward; the instantaneous steering responses; the chassis' composure and grip, ensuring fluent progress through the twisty stuff.

Although I took its dynamic thrills for granted, I was genuinely surprised by the Impreza's unimpeachable build quality. In nearly 28,000 miles in our care, Rex didn't develop a single squeak or rattle. It started first time, every time, and the only fault was the immobiliser sensor that detached itself from the A-pillar. No wonder the UK's pre-eminent customer satisfaction survey, run by J D Power and Associates, fêtes Subaru and its cars.

'TO MY EYES, NOTHING MATCHED ITS MIX OF PACE, GRIP, PINPOINT STEERING AND IMPECCABLE REFINEMENT'

OUR CARS

19 DECEMBER 2001

Volume 230

No 12 | 5465

AUTOCAR
Double issue
19/26 December 2001 £3.60

EXCLUSIVE DETAILS
NEW JAG
F-TYPE
Uncovered Britain's £30k mid-engined Boxster-beater

50 EXTRA PAGES
ROAD TEST YEAR BOOK
66 top new cars driven and rated

ROAD TEST YEARBOOK 2001

TESTED 200mph Merc SL Hot new Seat Ibiza
Best 911 ever Our Impreza at 30,000 miles
PLUS Don't laugh – it's the wind-powered car!

ABOVE McNamara pulls ahead of old-model Impreza as he rushes to the dealer for yet another service; attention every 7,500 miles is much too often.

But none of this gushing is to suggest that the WRX driving experience didn't irritate me at times. It did – whenever I was prised out of the car and shoehorned into anything else on the fleet. To my eyes, nothing matched its mix of pace, grip, pinpoint steering and impeccable refinement.

The Impreza isn't perfect, though. Editor Rob Aherne rightly reckoned the thin metal boot compared unfavourably with a Quality Street tin's lid. And how could Subaru forget a boot handle? The tinny stereo was widely condemned, particularly

for its minuscule removable security panel: a minor miracle it wasn't lost. The remote locking was infuriatingly unresponsive, too – you practically had to plip the button from inside to open the car. And the gearshift, though generally slick, was exceptionally reluctant to engage reverse.

More seriously, the headlamps weren't powerful enough, enforcing often tentative progress on B-roads at night. And the braking response deteriorated markedly, soon after 20k span round on the odometer. Although I was still proud of Rex's ultimate bite, the pedal began to feel spongy.

All this I could live with. However, two significant reservations would strongly influence my decision whether to buy a WRX or not. The first is the Mk2 Impreza's ugly, bug-eyed look. Soon after I took possession, a friend from Ford engineering arrived to sample the Impreza's delights. Having never seen the new car in the metal, his unsolicited reaction was telling – laughter. His verdict: the WRX's looks play right into the hands of the Focus RS, when eventually the Blue Oval's 217bhp Impreza-chaser actually makes it to the showrooms.

Later I polled my fiancée's opinion – of note,

SUBARU IMPREZA WRX

Car run for 10 months
Introduced in UK November 2000
Changes since then None to standard WRX mechanicals, equipment or price, although bigger brothers have entered the fold. The sold-out, rally-look UK300 paved the way for the STi, which arrives next month. This beefed-up bruiser wields an extra 46bhp, costs

a tempting £25,995 and is available with an optional £1,500 Prodrive bodykit.
UK sales to date 3,854
What makes it special? Simply an awesome drive. And if the Impreza feelgood factor wasn't already high enough, WRX STi driver Richard Burns has just been crowned England's first World Rally Champion.

because she was about to marry me and become eligible to drive the *Autocar* fleet (a decent dowry, perhaps). Despite my heady praise of Rex's dynamic abilities, her verdict was strong encouragement to bag deputy ed Hugo Andreae's beloved TT instead.

In fact the styling received no quarter wherever I turned. Sales of new Imprezas are static in the UK now, while women – who used to buy 50 per cent of Mk1 wagons – are rumoured to be barely giving the new car a second look.

However, looks are subjective and the WRX is a thing of beauty under the skin. My second reservation is more pertinent: its running costs.

Autocar staff racked up 27,536 miles in the WRX, at an average of 25.6 to the gallon. Now we would never claim our right feet suffer from weightlessness, especially when there's a turbocharged 2.0-litre boxer engine – capable of a 5.7sec sprint to 60mph – waiting to be uncorked. But our long-termer's performance, some 2.1mpg below the official combined figure, is unimpressive, especially given our high percentage of motorway miles.

Similarly priced rivals are more economical. Honda's 209bhp Accord Type-R manages 29.4mpg, while the all-wheel-drive Jaguar X-type officially squeezes 29.5mpg out of its 194bhp 2.5-litre V6.

Radio's removable security panel small enough to get lost in a deep pocket

Admittedly, both are only 2mpg better than the WRX's 27.7mpg, but over 60,000 miles that equates to a £400 saving. Over our 27,000-odd miles, thirsty Rex drank an estimated £3,668 of 98 octane. And with the 60-litre tank lasting just 255 miles on average, I was a familiar face at my local fuel station.

The irony is that the comfortable, refined WRX is now a fantastic motorway car, and tantalisingly in contention for high-mileage, eager drivers – until you consider its poor fuel economy and 242g/km of CO_2 per kilometre, which would land company drivers in the 30 per cent tax bracket.

While the WRX's appetite for fuel was lusty, its desire for servicing was insatiable. Currently, WRX service intervals are every 7,500 miles, so I found myself visiting Marlborough West London (020 8568 1414) roughly every three months. Of all the people I'd like to get on first name terms with (Michael Owen, Cindy Crawford...), service manager Dave Reading was not my first choice.

BELOW Selecting reverse gear only awkward part of WRX driving experience.

LOGBOOK IMPREZA WRX

TEST STARTED 03.11.01

Mileage at start	2,519
Mileage now	30,055

OPTION

Blue mica metallic paint	£250
Rally seats	£0 (no-cost option)

PRICES

List price new		£21,495
Total price new		£21,745
Value now:	Trade	£14,750
	Private	£15,500
	Retail	£16,500

FUEL CONSUMPTION

Govt urban	19.9mpg
Extra urban	35.8mpg
Combined	27.7mpg
Our test best	33.3mpg
Our test worst	16.3mpg
Our test average	25.6mpg

PERFORMANCE

Max speed	143mph
0–60mph	5.9sec
At 3,100 miles:	
0–30mph	2.0sec
0–40mph	3.1sec
0–50mph	4.3sec
0–60mph	5.7sec
0–70mph	7.8sec
0–80 mph	9.9sec
0–90 mph	12.8sec
0–100mph	16.9sec
30–50mph	4.3sec
50–70mph	9.6sec
Standing qtr mile	14.5sec/95mph
60–0mph	2.8sec
Top speed	141mph

SERVICING AND TYRES

7,500 miles	£138.99
Oil and filter change	
15,000 miles	£400.46
Oil and filter change, new brake pads	
22,500 miles	£127.76
Oil and filter change	
30,000 miles	£460.14 (est)
Oil and filter change, spark plugs, engine coolant, fuel and air filters, transmission and diff oil, brake fluid	
37,500 miles	£138.99 (est)
Oil and filter change	
45,000 miles	£191.76 (est)
Oil and filter change, spark plugs	
52,500 miles	£138.99 (est)
Oil and filter change	
60,000 miles	£718.48 (est)
Oil and filter change, spark plugs, engine coolant, fuel and air filters, transmission and diff oil, brake fluid, cam belt	

Labour rates (ex vat)
£62.50 per hour at Marlborough West London, Isleworth; £45.50 per hour at Beechdale Subaru, Derby.

Parts costs (excl VAT)
Air filter £19.76, spark plugs £10.72 each, oil filter £10.11, fuel filter £32.65, front brake pads £97.53, front bumper £119.37, rear bumper £107.33, alloy wheel £142.98, mirror assembly £139.40, headlamp £157.33.

Tyres Bridgestone Potenza 215/45 ZR17 – £115.67 each (incl VAT).

Monthly contract hire rate £370

COSTS OVER 27,500 MILES

Fuel	£3,668
Oil (non service)	£17.99
Service costs	£6,67.21
Repairs	Four tyres £490
Total running costs	£4,843.20
Running costs per mile	18p
Cost per mile (incl depreciation)	40p

INSURANCE (GROUP 19)

25-year-old single male, two speeding fines, five years' no-claims bonus, living in high-risk Manchester **£3,049**
35-year-old married male, clean licence, five years' no-claims bonus, living in low-risk Swindon **£1,483**

However, he and the Marlborough team performed admirably, providing courteous and quick service on every occasion.

At 7,500 miles, they changed the oil, gave Rex the once-over and left it in immaculate condition, for £138.99. Another oil change, coupled with replacement front brake pads, set me back £400.46 at 15,000 miles, while a further check up and top up at 22,500 miles cost £127.76. The servicing bill over 27,586 miles totalled £667.21.

According to motoring whole-life costs experts Henley Systems (www.topcalc.co.uk), an Impreza WRX driver will shell out £3120 on servicing, maintenance and repairs over 60,000 miles. The Accord Type-R will cost £1,612, the X-type £2,350.

Over 60,000 miles, Subaru recommends a WRX is serviced eight times, and that's excluding an initial lube at 1,000 miles. With the automotive equivalent of a personal fitness trainer, it's no wonder the Impreza performs so well in the J D Power reliability survey.

But such intensive monitoring is unacceptable and unnecessary. *Autocar*'s long-term turbocharged TT was first serviced at 18,000 miles – or three times over 60,000 miles. And while the Accord Type-R remains on a 9,000-mile cycle, Honda has since

boosted its schedule to every 12,000 miles for new models, including the Civic Type-R.

Subaru UK claims frequent checks are necessary because of their cars' high performance or off-road use. It doesn't wash. An Audi Allroad 2.7T Quattro has prescribed service intervals of 19,000 miles or every two years.

Subaru is likely to extend intervals in 2002, but I don't expect more than 10,000 miles between check-ups. And coming more than a year after mass manufacturers like Ford and Vauxhall dragged out their intervals to 20,000 miles, it's too little, too late.

So would I buy a Subaru Impreza WRX with my own money? In my first report, having been seduced by its dynamics, the answer was an emphatic 'yes'. But eight months later, my heart says yes, my head thinks maybe, but the pocket says no.

"Loved it but couldn't afford to run it," said the dealer of the WRX on the forecourt. So reads my epitaph for Rex, too.

ABOVE New car just as dynamic but more civilised than old Turbo.

BELOW LEFT Lots of hard driving but zero squeaks and rattles.

OUR VIEWS

This is such a great car, except for the terrible fuel economy and minuscule touring range. A classic motor – and my favourite on the fleet.
Rob Aherne

Over the B-roads of Wales, I realised how remarkable this car is. Damping and ride are superb, pedals are a delight. I think I even like the way it looks.
Chris Harris

My brother has a '97 Impreza and won't order this one on aesthetics alone. Otherwise he was impressed – astonishing improvement in refinement.
Patrick Fuller

The quality of the stereo and cupholders is the only let-down.
Ben Whitworth

SUBARU IMPREZA STi

IMPREZA STi TYPE UK Subaru's first UK-spec STi promises to be a much improved, more civilised all-rounder for British buyers. But will it be too tame for fans of the rally-bred saloon stormer?

There's no easy way of breaking this to you so we'll tell it straight. If you're expecting this, the UK-specification Subaru Impreza STi, to be a napalm-breathing, Evo VII-clubbing road warrior, the news is not good. On sale now for £25,995 (or £27,495 for the mechanically identical but visually yet more outrageous Prodrive version), the Euro-friendly 261bhp STi is necessarily somewhat watered down from the nominally 280bhp (and probably nearer 310bhp) domestic-specification STis that have slithered across these pages in recent months.

That's the bad news. The rather better news is that the STi has found another role for itself which, while less likely to grab the headlines, is equally compelling. And as we shall see, though its performance may have failed to make the advances you'd expect, the remaining improvements over the standard WRX more than justify the extra £4,500 outlay.

Besides, you'll still not mistake it for a slow car. Tuned by Subaru Tecnica International (hence STi), the quad-cam flat four, 2.0-litre powerplant retains just 20 per cent of the componentry featured on the standard 215bhp WRX. Totally revised cylinder heads with variable valve timing, shimless

QUICK FACTS

Model	Impreza STi Type UK
Price	£25,995
Top speed	148mph
30–70mph	4.7sec
0–60mph	4.9sec
60–0mph	3.1sec (damp)
MPG	22.7
For	Chassis, drivetrain, ride quality, refinement
Against	Poor economy, high emissions, too much understeer

ROAD TEST

16 JANUARY 2002

Volume 231

No 3 | 5468

ABOVE STi will understeer if you push it hard, but mostly it just grips and grips thanks to those 17in Bridgestones.

OPPOSITE Ride enhanced by chassis tweaks.

lifters and new valves take care of the top end while a reinforced block, forged pistons and beefed-up conrods make sure the bottom end stays in one piece amid the extra power. All told it

HISTORY

Given that it accounts for half of all Impreza sales today, it's a little hard to remember that, back at its 1994 UK launch, the Impreza Turbo was a very low volume niche product. Created first to homologate and then bathe in the reflected glory of Subaru's world rally car, the Impreza Turbo soon became a cult which showed no signs of diminishing. Many still-hotter versions have been created – the RB5, 22B, P1 and original WRX among them – but this STi is the first to have reached the UK neither as a limited edition special nor a grey import.

amounts to 261bhp at 6,000rpm and 253lb ft of torque at 4,000rpm.

But such promising figures prove only that you can prove anything with statistics. Tied to a car weighing all but a tonne-and-a-half, its power-to-weight ratio is reined back to a less spectacular 178bhp per tonne, or in other words, on a par with a stock Porsche Boxster. So it's quick but won't exactly wear out the road every time you put your foot down. Indeed our 0–60mph time of 4.9sec speaks more of all-wheel-drive traction than outright grunt, as the less impressive 0–100mph time of 13.5sec makes clear. All out it reaches 148mph, putting it in the BMW 330i bracket on the autobahn.

Not that you can expect 330i fuel consumption. Government calculations give a combined consumption of 23.3mpg, making the BMW's 31.0mpg appear sensationally frugal, and our experience with the Subaru bears this out.

ROAD TEST STi TYPE UK

MAXIMUM SPEEDS

6th 148mph/6,050rpm	5th 142/7,500
4th 103/7,500	3rd 79/7,500
2nd 58/7,500	1st 38/7,500

ACCELERATION FROM REST

True mph	seconds	speedo mph
30	1.7	30
40	2.5	40
50	3.4	51
60	4.9	61
70	6.4	71
80	8.4	82
90	10.7	92
100	13.5	102

Standing qtr mile 13.7sec/101mph

Standing km 25.9sec/125mph

30–70mph through gears 4.7sec

ACCELERATION IN GEAR

MPH	6th	5th	4th	3rd	2nd
20–40	-	10.9	6.3	5.8	2.4
30–50	15.0	8.9	4.5	4.3	1.9
40–60	14.2	7.3	3.3	3.0	-
50–70	12.3	5.5	3.3	2.5	-
60–80	8.7	4.6	3.6	2.7	-
70–90	8.0	5.4	4.2	-	-
80–100	8.6	6.3	5.3	-	-

FUEL CONSUMPTION

Average/best/worst/touring

22.7/24.0/12.7/24.0mpg

Urban/combined	16.9/23.3mpg
Extra urban	29.7mpg
Tank capacity	60 litres
Touring range	428 miles
CO_2	290g/km

BRAKES

30/50/70mph	9.8/25.6/50.1 metres
60–0mph	3.1sec

NOISE

Idle/max revs in 3rd 51/79dbA

30/50/70mph 68/71/74dbA

Overall it returned 22.7mpg in our hands, giving a real-world range of considerably less than 300 miles from its 13.2 gallon tank. A CO_2 emissions rating of 290g/km also means company buyers are clobbered with the full 35 per cent taxable liability. The BMW driver is assessed for tax on just 24 per cent of the list price.

Yet there is so much more to the Impreza's performance than is initially apparent. First, it has real character and it extends all the way from the smooth, quiet rasp of the flat four motor to the precision of its quick six-speed gearbox. The motor is tractable enough not to annoy at low revs, but show it 3,000rpm and it will surge forward with increasing urgency to a point still short of manic but firmly resident in the thrilling. In fact you only notice the monumental urge of the Japanese STi has absconded when, after 6,500rpm, this UK STi's power simply disappears. Home-sourced STis hit 8,000rpm like a battering ram at the castle doors.

Features like the pop-out cupholder feel a bit plasticky.

Cabin not the most stylish but it's all well laid-out.

Driver and passenger airbags are a standard fit.

ABOVE Well-placed instruments and controls make it a better driver's car.

But if provisos should be made about the STi's performance, its chassis needs no such qualification. With limited-slip differentials at both ends, inverted struts, beefed-up control arms, stiffer bushes and quicker steering, every area of the STi's chassis has received a first-class upgrade. And you'll know it before you're out of first gear because even the ride quality reeks of a sophistication you'd not normally credit to a four-door Japanese saloon suspended by those two pairs of inverted MacPherson struts. It's firm but as well damped as one of the better Porsches. It means that not only do you go about your business in comfort come what may, but also when it's time to really start travelling, you'll do so accompanied by some of the best body control around.

And in such conditions, the STi is at its brilliant best. Unlike an Evo VII, you don't need to be at light aircraft velocity and on a race track before it starts to excel. All you need is a bit of space.

Grip from its 225/45 ZR17 Bridgestone RE040 tyres is impressive in the dry and borderline astonishing when wet, while the steering points the car with an accuracy beyond what you should expect from a car of this weight. Push too hard and it will understeer a touch too strongly for our tastes, considering the four-wheel-drive set-up; nevertheless, a lift of the foot is not much to ask and that's almost always all that is required to restore your original line.

Fans of lurid oversteer will find it available but

WHAT IT COSTS

IMPREZA STi TYPE UK

On-the-road price	£25,995
Total as tested	£25,995
CO$_2$	290g/km
Cost per mile	73.9p
Contract hire/month	£533

INSURANCE

Insurance/typical quote	19/£1,511

WARRANTY

36 months/60,000 miles, 6 years anti-corrosion, 3 years' breakdown cover

EQUIPMENT CHECKLIST

Air conditioning	■
Metallic paint	£250
Prodrive upgrade	£1,500
Sat-nav	–
Electric seats	–
Leather seats	–
RDS stereo/CD player	■/■
Airbag driver/passenger	■/■
Alarm/immobiliser	■/■

■ = Standard na = not available

not on demand; you need to find somewhere safe, unsettle the car with a big lift early in the corner before getting back on the power as hard as you dare. Then the back will swing swiftly but predictably around, providing powerslides for the taking.

Subaru has also taken the time, at last, to equip its top-spec Impreza with decent brakes. Ventilated discs fill each golden 17in wheel rim and offer retardation that's great in the dry and, like the tyre grip, startling when wet. If only the hard pedal were not quite so lifeless.

The STi's true colours now emerge. Plant yourself behind the wheel and while you first notice the convincingly deep bucket seats, it is the sense of well-ordered cohesion that leaves the lasting impression. It all looks rather low rent but at least everything, from the geographical relationship of pedals, steering wheel, gearlever and driver to the minor controls, is where it should be.

There's not much room in the back but the boot is generous enough, making it a plausible carriage for a couple of youngish kids and their parents.

What really surprises, however, is its civility at speed. There's a little of everything at 85mph – wind, road and engine noise – but none is intrusive and, accompanied by well-judged gearing, that ride and excellent seats, it turns the STi into a long-distance cruiser of unlikely ability. Gentle pedal efforts, a good steering lock and clear extremities cope well with urban work, too.

It's built as you'd expect: there's not a material you'd mistake for one of true quality yet they come together to create a bomb-proof feeling. Even really shoddy fixtures like the pop-out cupholder in the dash fails to dent the impression that this, like every other Subaru, is one built for the long haul.

So the Impreza STi is not strictly an Evo VII rival. But while its abilities are not so deep, they have considerably greater breadth. Far from being a no-compromise tarmac-tearer, the STi is a superb all-rounder with no grave deficiencies and many laudable strengths. It is a better car than the standard WRX Impreza, even taking price into account.

As for the Evo VII, there's not a road tester among us who'd not rather drive the extraordinary Mitsubishi. But to buy and live with, year after year? As an only car, it would have to be the cheaper, more pragmatic and effective Subaru.

Not the quickest but the best Impreza yet ★★★★

SPECIFICATIONS STi TYPE UK

DIMENSIONS

Min/max front leg room 920/1,120mm Min/max rear leg room 640/850mm
Min/max front head room 920/1,110mm Interior width front/rear 1,430/1,430mm
Boot length 970mm Min/max boot width 960/1,340mm VDA boot volume na
Weight distribution front/rear 55/45 Width 1,990mm inc mirrors Kerb weight 1,470kg

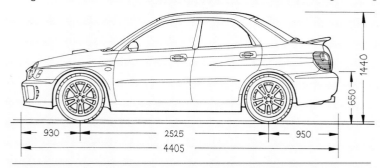

ENGINE

Layout	4 cyls horizontally opposed, 1,994cc
Max power	261bhp at 6,000rpm
Max torque	253lb ft at 4,000rpm
Specific output	131bhp per litre
Power to weight	178bhp per tonne
Torque to weight	172b ft per tonne
Installation	Front, in-line, four-wheel drive
Construction	Alloy head and block
Bore/stroke	92/75mm
Valve gear	4 per cyl, dohc
Compression ratio	8.0:1
Ignition and fuel	Electronic ignition, fuel injection, turbocharger

TRANSMISSION

Gearbox 6-speed manual
Ratios/mph per 1,000rpm
Final drive 3.90

1st	3.64/5.1	2nd	2.34/7.8
3rd	1.76/10.5	4th	1.35/13.7
5th	0.97/19.0	6th	0.76/24.5

STEERING

Type Rack and pinion, power assisted
Turns lock-to-lock 2.6
Turning circle 11.0m

CHASSIS AND BODY

Body	4dr saloon Cd 0.28
Wheels	7Jx17.5in
Tyres	225/45 ZR17 Bridgestone RE040
Spare	Semi space saver

SUSPENSION

Front Inverted MacPherson struts, coil springs, anti-roll bar
Rear Inverted MacPherson struts, trailing arm, dual link, coil springs, anti-roll bar

BRAKES

Front 330mm ventilated discs
Rear 305mm ventilated discs
Anti-lock Standard

PRODRIVE'S IMPREZA

Prodrive's performance package for the Impreza STi provides life-changing improvements over the standard car

When Subaru re-cast the Impreza Turbo in a slightly larger, more comfortable mould a couple of years ago, many thought the car's vital spark had been snuffed out. It was strange. Subjectively, the WRX's 215bhp felt more like 170bhp. It was as if the excitement gene had been surgically removed.

No need to panic, though. A performance car with a lineage that's as evolved, elongated and finely shaded in the name of customer satisfaction as the iconic Scooby's was never going to leave it at that. Like the old car, this new one has been hiked and spiked, both by the factory and its major motor sport partner. The 262bhp STi was a step in the right direction, but that magic word 'Prodrive' should supply the heat to fuse huge, supercar slashing performance with four-door usability. The mega-Scooby is back.

Prodrive's performance package for the STi basically comprises a re-programmed ECU, high-flow catalyst and sports exhaust system. The figures speak for themselves: 300bhp at 6,000rpm and 299lb ft of torque at 4,000rpm are life-changing improvements over the standard car's 262bhp and 253lb ft. Moreover, the substantially swollen outputs are delivered at exactly the same revs as the regular STi's, so the already impressive flexibility isn't compromised.

The Prodrive package costs £1,995 including fitting (£27,990 all up). It's also available on the facelifted car, shown at the British Motor Show and here next spring. There's no pressure to upgrade anything else – the standard STi can take it. But if the extra urge

QUICK FACTS

Model	Impreza STi Type UK Prodrive
Price	£27,500 (est)
On sale in UK	Now
0–62mph	4.6sec
Top speed	155mph

NEW CARS

30 OCTOBER 2002

Volume 234

No 5 | 5509

SPECIFICATIONS STi PRODRIVE

DIMENSIONS

Length	4,405mm
Width (inc mirrors)	1,990mm
Height	1,440mm
Wheelbase	2,525mm
Weight	1,470kg
Fuel tank	60 litres

ENGINE

Layout	Opposed four, 1,995cc
Max power	300bhp at 6,000rpm
Max torque	299lb ft at 4,000rpm
Power to weight	204bhp per tonne
Installation	Longitudinal, front, four-wheel drive
Bore/stroke	92.0mm/75.0mm
Made of	Aluminium alloy heads and block
Valve gear	4 per cyl
Ignition & fuel	Electronic ignition, IHI turbo, sequential injection

GEARBOX

Type 6-speed manual

SUSPENSION

Front Struts, coils, anti-roll bar
Rear Struts, coils, anti-roll bar

STEERING

Type Rack and pinion
Turns lock-to-lock 2.6

BRAKES

Front 330mm ventilated discs
Rear 305mm ventilated discs

WHEELS AND TYRES

Size 7Jx17.5in
Tyres 225/45 ZR17

THE **AUTOCAR** VERDICT

Just what the Scooby doctor ordered. Extra Prodrive pace sorts thrill factor and chassis balance. Remarkably good value

gives you the urge, you can opt for larger wheels and tyres, beefier brakes and suspension that's both lower and stiffer. We'd treat the last option with caution unless you've stuffed your diary with track days: the regular STi is amply low and stiff enough for the road. And that's how our test example arrived – purely and simply more powerful.

Fulsome as the normal STi's grunt is by new Scooby standards, in an all-out straight-line sprint it takes a pasting from the Prodrive version. The standard STi hits 60mph in 5.3sec, the Prodrive car in a claimed 4.6sec. It's the sort of gap that would be significant enough to notice on the road. Expect a good second and a half to be lopped off the 0–100mph time, too.

The main difference is that the regular STi only begins to feel genuinely rapid past 4,000rpm. It's mid-to-upper range attack is exceptional, but its low-to-mid tug leaves something to be desired. Serious action in the Prodrive starts earlier and is sustained longer. To mix a couple of cliches, the STi punches its weight but it's the Prodrive that has the killer instinct. Its mid-range rush is massive but, crucially, doesn't tail off. The Prodrive engine feels as if it has larger lungs and a harder, hungrier demeanour.

And it's much more rewarding to use in anger. In the zone, it recalls the legendary fast Scoobies of old like the P1, its uniquely gruff, flat-four backbeat (though with fewer of the extravagant turbo whoops, whistles and sighs) orchestrated beautifully by the closely stacked ratios of the six-speed 'box with its snappy, short-throw gearchange.

This car has frankly gobsmacking overtaking shove and so much torque it's seldom necessary to slot anything lower than fourth. Big-time brakes, too, with massive retardation on call and super-firm, top-of-the-pedal feel – not too sensitive on initial application and therefore easy to modulate, especially when you're heeling and toeing. They inspire heaps of confidence.

Likewise the four-wheel-drive chassis. The standard STi appears to have all the stability and grip in the world. Maybe unnecessarily so. The Prodrive's 300bhp gives it a bit more stick, though, and it's all to the good.

On a twisting road there's little that can live with a standard STi, so you may consider the extra firepower an extravagance. Go and grip are prodigious and well matched; you can takes liberties with the car and not frighten yourself. It strikes a very respectable balance between entertainment and safety.

But the Prodive makes you painfully aware of what you've been missing. It's as if its chassis was only being allowed to work within a restricted framework. In

short, the extra power seems to exert considerable influence on the precision with which the nose can be placed; apexes that would have been narrowly missed can be deftly brushed time after time. It feels as planted to the road as any car on earth, but so much more biddable than the STi.

So a 911 Turbo for a third of the price? Slightly diluted pace and grip not-withstanding, it does much the same kind of thing. It's faster, braver, stronger and more talented than most of the people who will drive it. It simply achieves more for a given input.

Better still, it really responds to being taken by the scruff of the neck. And you can have a riot doing it. If you're a Scooby fan this is just about as good as it currently gets. Much the same thing can be said of the Mitsubishi Evo VII, of course, except that the Scooby is a somewhat more friendly proposition on the limit and even the Prodrive doesn't feel quite as maniacally fast as the Evo.

If you're a Scooby newcomer, though, make sure you're fully acquainted with the deal. Supercar straightline performance meets advanced all-drive grip and traction, means that very little is quicker

from A to B. But fun as it is, getting the best out of it is a fairly brutal business. But if you're not nailing it, the driving experience can be less than spellbinding. Not quite all or nothing, but back off and you'll search in vain for incidental charms.

ABOVE Prodrive puts Impreza back with the best; digs deeper and at lower revs without over-stretching chassis.

LEFT Bug-eyed lights soon to change.

OPPOSITE interior still rather ho-hum, but standard brakes and steering are terrific.

SCOOBY DOES

People didn't just dislike the look of the Impreza, they stopped buying it. Hence the reason the 2003 car is more than just a pretty face

According to its creators the new-look Subaru Impreza has "a more aggressive looking, yet more aerodynamic, front end". Which is probably just as well in the overall scheme of things. The current Scooby, launched over here only two years ago, may well have been as sweet to drive as any £20k car but, visually, it was more Marilyn Manson than Marilyn Monroe.

And the scariest part for Subaru was that, eventually, people began voting against the bug-ugly Impreza with their wallets: they stopped buying it and started looking elsewhere for their thrills.

The good news is that Subaru clearly listens to its critics, and has reacted accordingly – with some haste. Thanks largely to the work of Brit designer Peter Stevens, also responsible for such classics as the McLaren F1, Lotus Elan and, more recently, the MG SV coupé, the new Scooby has a much more handsome face.

The STi version we drove, and which you see here, still has the obligatory collection of scoops and ducts, each designed to channel air to a specific moving part beneath the skin. But the overall effect is of a far smoother, more appealing shape. So if the public begins to reappear at dealers' doors when the car goes on sale next February, it will be Stevens who Subaru should thank.

Mechanically, the new Impreza continues virtually unaltered. The front suspension bushes have been uprated and a new bracing strut has been added between the front suspension turrets. There are also new bushes on the lower arms at the front.

QUICK FACTS

Model	Subaru Impreza STi
Price	£27,500 (est)
On sale in UK	February
0–62mph	5.1sec
Top speed	150mph

FIRST DRIVE

13 NOVEMBER 2002

Volume 234

No 7 | 5511

ABOVE New nose is much better looking than before. Chassis is sweeter but engine has no more power.

Fundamentally, however, it's a case of 'we know it ain't broke so we didn't bother fixing it'.

In essence there's been a slight reduction in geometry change under hard cornering which, says Subaru, improves the high-speed body control. But on

UK VS JAPAN

What's the difference between a UK-spec and a Jap-spec Impreza?

Quite a lot really. For starters the Jap cars have more powerful engines due to the stricter Euro emission regs that UK cars have to pass. A Jap-spec WRX has over 240bhp and the STi 276bhp. In the UK, post Euro 3 regs, these outputs fall to 215bhp and 261bhp. We also don't get the lightweight Spec C STi over here in any form, which is a real pity because it has even less turbo lag and, apparently, an even more aggressive chassis set-up than the regular STi. Conclusion: if you can afford to, and you have the patience to wait, go for the 300bhp Prodrive upgrade if you really want your Scooby to go.

the road you'd be hard pushed to notice the difference, beyond a gentle stiffening of the ride at low speed.

Similarly, performance over the outgoing models is marginally improved – on both regular WRX and STi versions – but only because the new widescreen bonnet scoop allows more air to be rammed into the massive intercooler nestling beneath. There's also a change to the shape of the intercooler water-spray nozzle and a revised baffle inside the air scoop, again to ensure that the maximum amount of air reaches the radiator.

Internally, the engines are unchanged, which means 215bhp for the WRX, 261bhp for the STi and a full 300bhp for the factory-sanctioned Prodrive STi. Like the engine, the gearbox is carried over unfettled: six-speed for the STi, five for the WRX.

Encouragingly, Subaru has also reacted to criticism of the car's cabin, never its strongest suit. Huge all-embracing bucket seats with pink STi logos continue to dominate the cabin in the top-spec model. But up front there are a number of welcome improvements in both variants, including a revised centre console, new instruments, whiplash-reducing head restraints, Isofix rear child-seat mounts and a new energy-absorbing brake pedal which, according to Subaru, is designed to snap under a heavy impact.

The most obvious interior change is the fitment of a smaller Momo steering wheel, which looks and feels great compared with the salver-sized items of previous Scoobys.

Outside, Subaru claims that the new STi model is more stable, thanks to its bigger rear wing. No downforce figures are available, but the new front and rear spoilers are said to improve stability above 65mph and make the STi look even more like a caricature of a WRC car.

Whatever minuscule extra amount of horsepower may have been liberated by the revised intercooling – officially there is no more power available but unofficially all versions feel quicker in the real world – it's hard to detect a great deal of difference on the road. Not that the STi exactly wants for performance. In truth the new car goes like the old one did on a cold day with the strongest brew of super unleaded in the tank.

Over the pock-marked Japanese roads west of Mt Fuji that we drove on, the combination of firmer suspension and the typically laggy delivery of the STi engine conspired to make it feel typically exciting, if a little frantic in ride terms.

The steering works hard to self-centre when you're merely pottering, but as the speed builds up, so the weight of response adjusts, and you can start to enjoy a sublimely balanced chassis whose greatest strengths remain mighty suspension control and immense grip at each corner. Despite the suspension tweaks the STi is still, in extremis, an understeerer, but you need to be travelling so quickly to discover this that, on the road, it's just not an issue to get concerned about.

The more important news is that Subaru has at least tried to close the gap between the Impreza and Evo when it comes to feedback, most obviously through the steering, but also through the seats. No, the new Scooby does not dart in whichever direction your wrists flick it like an Evo does, but it's certainly more go-kart-like than it was. In a car like this, that has to be a step forward, despite the ride being rather busier.

So has Subaru done enough to stop the sales rot and make people start buying Imprezas again? That's up to you, of course. But if a car that looks better, goes fractionally harder and handles more sharply is what was required, you can't accuse Subaru of not delivering. On this evidence the new Scooby is everything it needed to be, and more.

SPECIFICATIONS IMPREZA STi

DIMENSIONS

Length	4,405mm
Width (inc mirrors)	1,990mm
Height	1,440mm
Wheelbase	2,525mm
Weight	1,470kg
Fuel tank	60 litres

ENGINE

Layout	Flat four, 1,998cc, turbocharged
Max power	261bhp at 6,000rpm
Max torque	253lb ft at 4,000rpm
Specific output	131bhp per litre
Power to weight	178bhp per tonne
Installation	Front, in line, 4wd
Bore/stroke	92.0/75.0mm
Made of	Alloy head and block
Compression ratio	8.0:1
Valve gear	4 per cyl, dohc
Ignition and fuel	Electronic ignition, sequential injection, IHI turbo

SUSPENSION

Front Struts, coils, anti-roll bar
Rear Struts, coils, anti-roll bar

ECONOMY

Combined mpg	23.3mpg

GEARBOX

Type 6-speed manual
Ratios/mph per 1,000rpm
Final drive 3.90

1st 3.64/5.1		2nd 2.34/7.8	
3rd 1.76/10.5		4th 1.35/13.7	
5th 0.97/19.0		6th 0.76/24.5	

STEERING

Type Rack and pinion
Turns lock-to-lock 2.6

BRAKES

Front 330mm ventilated discs
Rear 305mm ventilated discs

WHEELS AND TYRES

Size 7.0Jx17in
Made of Alloy
Tyres 225/45 ZR17 Bridgestone RE040

THE **AUTOCAR** VERDICT

Better looking, more exciting to drive and quicker. The war of the Evos continues

SUBARU IMPREZA STi

IMPREZA STi TYPE UK We put the latest UK-spec STi through its paces to see if it can reclaim the ground lost by the previous, short-lived incarnation of Subaru's rally-racer

Rarely has car hi-fi been as superfluous to a car's needs as it is in the new Impreza STi. That the unit itself sounds apologetic when the car is stationary and is inaudible on even the lightest throttle openings just doesn't matter because – and this is where impatience forces me to break with tradition and tell you what I think of it at such an early stage in proceedings – I think it might be the only aspect of this car that isn't spot on. Particularly as this car runs the Subaru-approved 300bhp Prodrive tweak.

You probably already know the paradox of the outgoing Type UK STi: in name and image it was a supposedly uncompromising rally-racer riddled with compromises. Significantly less powerful than Japanese-spec cars to satisfy Euro 3 emissions regulations, it offered only 262bhp (instead of the full 300). Still, it should have commanded waiting lists. But didn't.

Prodrive did the decent thing and bumped the power up to 300bhp, but by then the damage was done and, anyhow, however many ponies you extracted from the engine, the styling presented the biggest barrier to strong sales. Which is why just one year after the last Type UK STi was launched, we have a revised car.

That it carries the same name as before, is significantly cheaper, better looking and enjoys a generous wave of small detail changes won't fill those that paid for the 2002 product with joy. And just how much profit was being made per unit

QUICK FACTS

Model	Subaru Impreza STi Type UK (300bhp)
Price	£26,990
On sale	February
0–62mph	4.6sec
Top speed	155mph

NEW CARS

29 JANUARY 2003

Volume 235

No 5 | 5521

when you can afford to make such revisions and charge just £24,995 for the end product (a £1k saving) is probably worth considering, but not dwelling upon, because the STi has become a bargain.

So popular was the Prodrive conversion on last year's car that the company doesn't actually have a 262bhp version on its test fleet. In exchange for £1995 and two-and-a-half hours of your time at the dealer, Subaru will boost your STi's vitals to a solid 300bhp at 6,000rpm and 299lb ft of torque at 4,000rpm. No more powerful than before, but then something that claims a 0–60mph charge in 4.6sec and 100mph in 12.2sec doesn't need much more poke. And I'm sure that 100mph time is beatable.

You decide what you think of the new clothing and I'll just run through the alterations. Redesigned bumpers incorporating new light units perk its face and rump, different side skirts and the standard fitment of that enormous rear spoiler (previously an option) complete a visual link with Mr Mäkinen's rally version that's as tangible as we've seen for years. The bonnet's more steeply raked, the air scoop has a mouth to shame a basking shark and the front wings are even more pumped. Believe me: in the flesh, in black, it does the trick.

Underskin tweaks have been reserved for the suspension and steering. All four MacPherson struts are now mounted upside-down to improve geometry under load and both sets of bushes have been uprated. Stronger mounts for the front struts, redesigned rear units and extra scaffolding for the rear crossmember create a more rigid platform and should contribute to a sharper drive. Both axles now benefit from a limited-slip differential, where before only the rear had one.

But if one component telegraphs the change in character of this car it's the revised steering rack. Leaned-down to 2.6 turns and working through a smaller wheel, it's the defining factor in a car that feels significantly more purposeful on the road and in character draws it much closer to Mitsubishi's frenetic Evo. The single factor that made the old STi seem slightly aloof at times, the lag between driver input and vehicle response, has been hacked away mercilessly.

I love the fact that it feels turbocharged, not so breathless below 3,000rpm that it pinks and flounders (it's actually a reasonable lugger), but because Subaru hasn't tried to dilute the thrill of forced induction; I love hearing the faint tweet of blower spooling up before it fires you up the road. That point comes at 3,000rpm, nuts your head against the seat and doesn't relent until 7,000rpm. No matter what the road conditions, the efforts of every pony go unwasted, too: the traction is amazing. Downsides are the now-traditional Scooby stutter when pulling away from rest and a transmission that still doesn't like to be hurried.

But the chassis's a gem. Far more aggressive in its responses, and all the more honest for it. The ride quality has suffered, but the trademark damper control that makes these cars so usable in the UK remains. Its chassis remains neutral for longer and is less inclined to oversteer on a trailing throttle, but the front end is significantly more accurate than it was thanks to the quicker steering.

Nothing much has changed inside: blue faced dials, slightly different trim, smaller wheel: that's about it. But the fundamentals in something this fast are crucial and the STi's seats, driving position and pedals are excellent.

For the money only the forthcoming Evo VIII will come close, and that seems to have undergone the reverse styling process to become uglier than before. But where the Subaru really scores is in offering an entire world of extra performance over the hot-hatch brigade, and therefore an honest graduation point. It's a very fast, entertaining and fine-looking car that happens to be far cheaper than before. Even if the hi-fi is shoddy.

SPECIFICATIONS STi TYPE UK

ECONOMY

Urban	18.2mpg
Extra urban	33.2mpg
Combined	25.4mpg
CO_2 emissions	na

DIMENSIONS

Length	4,415mm
Width	1,950mm
Height	1,440mm
Wheelbase	2,525mm
Weight	1,470kg
Fuel tank	60 litres

ENGINE

Layout	Flat four, 1,994cc, turbo
Max power	300bhp at 6,000rpm
Max torque	299lb ft at 4,000rpm
Specific output	151bhp per litre
Power to weight	204bhp per tonne
Installation	Longitudinal, front, four-wheel drive
Bore/stroke	92.0 x 75.0mm
Compression ratio	8.0:1
Valve gear	4 per cyl, dohc per bank
Ignition and fuel	Electronic ignition, sequential injection, IHI turbo

All figures are manufacturer's claims

SUSPENSION

Front Inverted struts, coil springs, anti-roll bar
Rear Inverted struts, coil springs, anti-roll bar

GEARBOX

Type 6-speed manual
Ratios/mph per 1,000rpm
Final drive ratio 3.90

1st 3.64/5.1		2nd 2.38/7.8	
3rd 1.76/10.5		4th 1.35/13.7	
5th 0.97/19.0		6th 0.76/24.5	

STEERING

Type Rack and pinion, power-assisted
Turns lock-to-lock 2.6

BRAKES

Front 330mm ventilated discs
Rear 305mm ventilated discs

WHEELS AND TYRES

Size 7.5J x 17in
Tyres 225/45 ZR17 Bridgestone Potenza RE 040

THE **AUTOCAR** VERDICT

More fun for less cash and a decent set of clothes at last. This might be the car to unseat the new Evo VIII.

SUBARU IMPREZA WRX

IMPREZA WRX 5-DOOR Two years and one face-lift later, the Impreza is back. It has a neater styling and the performance is up, but this time around the competition is ready

A decade is a long time at the top, something Subaru is acutely aware of right now. When the first Impreza Turbo arrived in 1994 it forced us to adjust our notion of the affordable performance car, much as the Sierra Cosworth had a decade earlier, and the Golf GTi 10 years before that. On rally stages, the high street and computer screens, the iconic Impreza captured the hearts and wallets of enthusiasts like no other Japanese car before and put Subaru on the map in the UK.

But no one could have predicted that Subaru would help to slay its own golden goose. We could have lived with the weaker performance of the second-generation car in return for the improvements in refinement and driveability, but the aesthetic crimes were less forgivable. Within months of the bug-eyed Mk2's arrival, rumours of declining sales and a hasty re-skin were rife. Just two years on – less than a third of the life span of the Mk1 – the restyled Scooby is here, challenging the new breed of 200bhp super hatches that are now on forecourts as well.

DESIGN AND ENGINEERING ★★★★★
No big surprises. Sound, proven engineering

Job one: fixing those headlights. We never warmed to the previous car's styling. More important, neither did

QUICK FACTS

Model tested	WRX 5-door
List price	£20,495
Top speed	140mph
30–70mph	5.8sec
0–60mph	5.5sec
70–0mph	48.3m
MPG	23.0
For	Performance, ride, traction, steering
Against	Drab interior

ROAD TEST

29 JANUARY 2003

Volume 235

No 5 | 5521

AUTOCAR

20 EXTRA PAGES

BRITAIN'S BEST TYRES
- Name a Porsche faster than an M3
- How to turn £65 on new tyres
- Increase your car's speed and safety

PLUS Can we have this Capri please Ford?
We resurrect the legend

NEW VOLVO BEATS BMW
4x4 MEGA TEST How radical new XC90 redefines the 4x4

SCOOBY SPECIAL
- New WRX –
full road test
- Bag a bargain
used Impreza
- New STi driven

ABOVE Cabin is a genuine five-seater plus luggage room, although boot space is compromised by suspension.

RIGHT Same wings are carried over from previous model.

you to judge by the sales. Subaru's solution? Bring back some of the flavour of the original Impreza. The result, while hardly beautiful, is a definite improvement on the outgoing car's Pikachu face. The new, inwardly sloping, scowling lamps deliver a far more aggressive presence but, more important, one that is instantly recognisable as an Impreza, markedly resembling the last of the first-generation cars. The rest of the exterior styling is largely carried over although there have been tweaks to the bumpers and rear lights, and that famous bonnet scoop is also bigger. As before, the five-door

WRX uses the standard unflared wings, unlike its hot four-door siblings.

When the last car was launched we concluded that, styling aside, there was precious little wrong with the WRX. So the design team could have fixed the face and left it at that. But two years ago there was no Civic Type-R, no Focus RS and no Golf R32 – so this time Subaru couldn't afford to rest on its laurels.

Lucky, then, that it had such fine materials from which to work, including the charismatic turbocharged flat-four engine. Changes to the power unit aren't groundbreaking but reprogramming the ECU and fitting sodium-filled valves, lighter valve springs and retuning the engine to run on 97-octane fuel has produced a more powerful motor that consumes less fuel and emits less CO_2. Peak power climbs from 215bhp to 222bhp at 5,600rpm (a 95-octane power figure isn't quoted but it won't be 222bhp) while torque grows from 215lb ft to 221, but produced 400rpm higher at 4,000rpm. The CO_2 figure drops to 219g/km against 242g/km for the old model – knocking five per cent off next year's tax liability.

Under normal conditions the engine drives all four wheels equally, a centre differential with a viscous coupling dividing power between the front and rear axles, just as before. The rear axle is fitted with a limited-slip device, but the front, unlike the higher-powered STi model, is not.

Stiffening the floorpan of the new car means the saloon is apparently 250 per cent more resistant to bending than before, the hatchback 239 per cent, which Subaru claims improves crash safety, ride and handling. Other dynamic tweaks include a revised pump for the speed-sensitive power steering system to enhance stability and, on the saloon, a 20mm track increase. The MacPherson strut front and trailing-arm rear set-up is retained, but both springs and dampers have been revised: the springs are marginally stiffer than they were and the dampers are of a higher specification. Subaru has also slightly altered the suspension pick-up points, again to ensure increased control of wheel movement.

The 294mm front and 266mm ventilated rear discs are carried over unchanged but now come with Electronic Brakeforce Distribution as standard.

PERFORMANCE/BRAKES ★★★★★
WRX claws back lost ground

Bug-eyed looks aside, one of the main criticisms levelled at the outgoing Impreza was that it had less kick than the previous-generation car, a problem that became even more apparent as the rush of cheaper 200bhp hatches flooded onto the market. But although the changes to power and torque are minor on the 2003 Impreza, they have resulted in a slight but significant improvement in performance.

With swift use of the sweet five-speed gearbox and some brutal clutch abuse to maximise the benefits of the four-wheel-drive system, the Impreza rockets off the line, hitting 30mph in just 1.9sec, leaving its front-drive rivals scrabbling in its wake as it demolishes 60mph in 5.5sec and 100mph in 16.1sec.

Those times are a definite improvement on last year's car's, which in lighter, four-door guise, took 5.7sec to hit 60mph and 16.9sec to reach the tonne, and the Focus RS which needs 6.3sec and 16.4sec respectively. But relieved of its off-the-line handicap, the Focus always feels the quicker of the two. Its 30–70mph time of 5.8sec is a small but significant 0.2sec quicker.

A look at the in-gear numbers uncovers another minor chink in the WRX's armour. Prod the right pedal with less than 3,000rpm on the dial and you'll be met with little in the way of forward thrust. Flexibility has improved slightly: the lug from

ROAD TEST IMPREZA WRX

MAXIMUM SPEEDS
5th 140mph/5,670rpm **4th** 136/7,250
3rd 97/7,250 **2nd** 67/7,250
1st 38/7,250

ACCELERATION FROM REST

True mph	seconds	speedo mph
30	1.9	32
40	2.9	42
50	4.1	53
60	5.5	63
70	7.7	74
80	9.7	84
90	12.5	95
100	16.1	106
110	19.9	116
120	26.5	127

Standing qtr mile 14.3sec/95mph
Standing km 27.0sec/121mph
30–70mph through gears 5.8sec

ACCELERATION IN GEAR

MPH	5th	4th	3rd	2nd
20–40	16.6	9.4	5.2	2.9
30–50	14.1	7.6	3.9	2.4
40–60	11.9	6.0	3.5	2.6
50–70	9.5	5.2	3.6	-
60–80	8.0	5.4	3.8	-
70–90	8.6	5.9	4.8	-
80–100	10.0	6.4	-	-

FUEL CONSUMPTION
Average/best/worst/touring
23.0/35.2/11.1/28.4mpg

Urban/combined	22.2/30.7mpg
Tank capacity	60 litres
Touring range	375 miles
CO_2	219g/km

BRAKES
30/50/70mph 9.1/24.3/48.3 metres
60–0mph 3.0sec

NOISE
Idle/max revs in 3rd 44/80dbA
30/50/70mph 62/69/74dbA

TESTER'S NOTES
Good to find the volume control for the new stereo on the right nearer the driver, although wheel-mounted buttons would be better. **Chris Chilton**

Maybe it was the unassuming five-door shell, but few other road users seemed to notice that this was the new Impreza. **Ben Oliver**

Subaru has squeezed more power out of the engine on 97-octane fuel. But what about on 95, which is what most people use? **Steve Sutcliffe**

SPECIFICATIONS IMPREZA WRX

DIMENSIONS

Min/max front leg room 820/1,080mm Min/max rear leg room 590/860mm
Min/max front head room 880/960mm Interior width front/rear 1,470/1,450mm
VDA boot volume 356/1,266 litres/dm³ Min/max boot length 910/1,670mm
Boot width 970/1,480mm Boot height 430mm Front/rear tracks 1,465/1,455mm
Weight distribution front/rear 59/41 Width 1,950mm inc mirrors Kerb weight 1,410kg

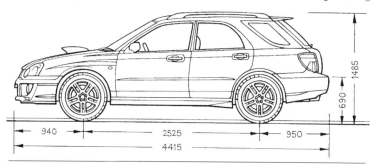

1485 | 690 | 940 | 2525 | 950 | 4415

ENGINE

Layout	4 cyl boxer, 1,994cc
Max power	222bhp at 5,600rpm
Max torque	221lb ft at 4,000rpm
Specific output	111bhp per litre
Power to weight	157bhp per tonne
Torque to weight	157lb ft per tonne
Installation	Front, longitudinal, 4wd
Construction	Alloy block & heads
Bore/stroke	92.0/75.0mm
Valve gear	4 per cyl, dohc
Compression	ratio 8.0:1
Ignition and fuel	Sequential multi-point fuel injection, turbo, petrol

TRANSMISSION

Gearbox 5-speed manual
Ratios/mph per 1,000rpm
Final drive 3.9

1st 3.45/5.3	2nd 1.95/9.4
3rd 1.37/13.4	4th 0.94/18.8
5th 0.74/24.7	

CHASSIS AND BODY

Body	5-door hatch Cd 0.37
Wheels	7Jx17in, alloy
Tyres	215/45 ZR17
	Bridgestone RE050

STEERING

Type Rack and pinion hydraulic assistance
Turns lock-to-lock 2.8
Turning circle 11.0m

SUSPENSION

Front Independent MacPherson struts and coil springs, transverse link, anti-roll bar

Rear Independent, MacPherson struts, trailing arms, coil springs, anti-roll bar

BRAKES

Front 294mm ventilated discs
Rear 266mm ventilated discs
Anti-lock Standard

THE SMALL PRINT © Autocar 2003. For further information on the Impreza WRX contact Subaru UK Ltd, Ryder Street, West Bromwich, West Midlands B70 OEJ (08705 100568). The cost-per-mile figure is calculated over three years/36,000 miles and includes depreciation, maintenance, road tax, funding and fuel, but not insurance. Figure supplied by Fleet Management Services (01743 241121). The insurance quote is for a 35-year-old professional male with a clean licence and full no-claims bonus, living in Swindon, supplied by What Car? Insurance. Contract hire figure is based on a lease for three years/36,000 miles, includes maintenance and is supplied by Lombard (0870 902 3311).

30–50mph in fourth now takes 7.6sec instead of 8.0sec but an Astra GSi is quicker still at 7.3sec. All out it reached 140mph, 3mph shy of Subaru's claim.

As expected the brakes are excellent having strong pedal feel and stopping distances just a fraction longer than the RS's.

However you cut it, the latest WRX is still a seriously quick car and more than capable of holding its own against the new generation of super hatches.

HANDLING AND RIDE ★★★★★
Outstanding grip and all-weather security

Short of climbing straight from an old car into the new, it is initially hard to detect any significant changes between the two on the road – and that's no bad thing. The outgoing car was, after all, a benchmark sports saloon and only the arrival of the Focus RS has called the validity of that title into question. We hailed the Ford as the new champ after a memorable moors thrash last year, but stepping back into the WRX reminded us again just what a difficult decision it had been to make.

New hi-fi looks better but stills sounds cheap beside rival units.

Excellent, delicate steering is communicative, doesn't load up.

Instruments have smart silver surrounds.

All the dynamic qualities that endeared us to the WRX two years ago remain intact, not least the beautifully delicate steering. At 2.7 turns it's on the slow side for a modern performance car and it can take time to acclimatise to the subtle messages being transmitted from the front wheels. But you soon warm to its strengths, including its refusal to load up no matter what you throw at it.

Then there's the impeccable damping that smooths out the worst Britain's craggy B-roads can deliver while allowing just enough information through to the driver. Even a 300-mile motorway marathon is treated with the sort of disdain that most rivals reserve solely for A and B roads. And let's not forget the fantastic all-weather traction, something the Focus RS would kill for. For some though, the edgier Ford will still be first choice. It hasn't the Subaru's breadth of ability, but confronted with a twisting ribbon of dry tarmac we'd still take the RS. Whether you could live with a car like this on a day-to-day basis is a matter of opinion. Opting for the WRX's marginally less frenetic approach to life should certainly not be seen as accepting second best.

SAFETY AND EQUIPMENT ★★★★★
Practical, unexceptional

Subaru has never quite perfected the art of making decent car interiors, but the minor changes made to the new car are certainly a positive step. Subtle tweaks including repositioning the rev-counter

OPPOSITE Rev counter has been repositioned to centre of dash; CD comes as standard but sound quality is poor.

WHAT IT COSTS

SUBARU IMPREZA WRX

			EQUIPMENT CHECKLIST	
On-the-road price	£20,495		Air conditioning	■
Price as tested	£20,495		17-inch alloy wheels	■
CO$_2$	219g/km		Four electric windows	■
Cost per mile	67.4p (est)		Alarm and immobiliser	■
Contract hire/month	£440 (est)		Metallic paint	£250
			CD player	■
INSURANCE			Sports seats	■
Insurance/typical quote	18/£1,289		Front/side airbags	■/■

WARRANTY
3 yrs/60,000 miles, 6 yrs anti-corrosion

■ = Standard na = not available

THE CLASS

SUBARU IMPREZA WRX 5-DOOR £20,495 ★★★★

Capacity 1,994cc
Power 222bhp
Torque 221lb ft
0–60mph 5.5sec
Max speed 140mph
CO_2 219g/km

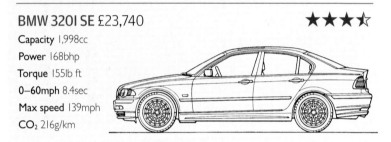

Forget the restyled headlamps, the biggest change to the Impreza is the effect running one will have on your pocket. It's quicker, too, and still unbeatable as a car for all seasons, but rivals have closed the gap.

BMW 320I SE £23,740 ★★★★☆

Capacity 1,998cc
Power 168bhp
Torque 155lb ft
0–60mph 8.4sec
Max speed 139mph
CO_2 216g/km

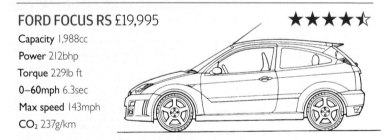

Something of a fish out of water in this company, but if you're prepared to sacrifice outright performance for outright finesse and build quality, this is where you'll come. Creamy six is green but light on torque.

FORD FOCUS RS £19,995 ★★★★★☆

Capacity 1,988cc
Power 212bhp
Torque 229lb ft
0–60mph 6.3sec
Max speed 143mph
CO_2 237g/km

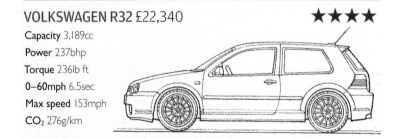

Divides opinion like euro discussions at Tory/Labour Party conferences. Finally toppled the Impreza in a group test last year and holds off the new one for thrills, but some drivers will find it asks too much.

VOLKSWAGEN R32 £22,340 ★★★★

Capacity 3,189cc
Power 237bhp
Torque 236lb ft
0–60mph 6.5sec
Max speed 153mph
CO_2 276g/km

R32 is a real surprise: the best Golf in over a decade and a worthy foil for the Focus RS. Chassis is a peach as is the snarly V6 but dead steering, a stiff list-price and high emissions lose it vital Brownie points.

STi-style in the centre of the dash, circling the dials with a dash of silver and adding a new radio facia are all welcome, although the hi-fi's sound quality remains as dreadful as ever. Standard kit levels are reasonably high and include a CD player, air conditioning and four electric windows, but sat-nav is still not available, even as an option.

In practical terms, though, there's little to complain about. The cabin is roomy enough for five, the driving position is near-perfect despite the wheel adjusting for rake only and, of course, in five-door form, the WRX has the advantage of an estate body shell and split-folding rear seats denied the saloon.

This plus is to some extent compromised by the Impreza's chassis and running gear: the rear suspension towers protrude awkwardly into the boot and the rear axle position pushes the load sill and boot floor up far higher than they would be in a conventional front-wheel-drive hatch.

Yet it's still more spacious than a smaller regular hatch such as the Focus. Push those rear seats flat and you will also open up 1,266 litres of cargo area that transforms the WRX into a genuinely useful load carrier, if not one as roomy as a genuine estate such as an Audi A4 Avant.

Safety and security levels have also been improved. Two front airbags remain standard, but the passenger bag is now dual-stage while side airbags become standard for the first time on the WRX. Deadlocks and special lock shields have also been fitted to keep the light-fingered at bay.

ECONOMY ★★★★★
Much better, but still thirsty if provoked

Given the greater performance and slight increase in weight, we were pleasantly surprised to find the Impreza more frugal than the old car. In theory, a small turbocharged engine should be far more economical than a large normally aspirated one when used sensibly, but the Impreza's infectious nature combined with a frustrating paucity of bottom-end grunt means you'll need the patience of a saint to get near the 30.7mpg official combined figure in everyday driving. But after recording 11.1mpg at the test track we did manage an excellent 35.2mpg on one particularly conscientious motorway trip, and although our 23.0mpg average seems low, it represents a huge improvement over the 18.7mpg we recorded last time out, and delivers a 300-mile-plus range.

MARKET & FINANCE ★★★★★
Finally, the sums add up

Deep pockets were always required for Impreza ownership, but Subaru has tried hard to soften the blow. The new sub-£20k starting price for the saloon (£20,495 for the wagon tested here) and improved economy will be much appreciated, but the 23g/km drop in CO_2 to 219g/km should transform the WRX's appeal to the company car driver, saving a 40 per cent tax-payer nearly £600 every year.

Bosses hope that the security improvements will net a drop in premiums although no official group rating was available at the time of writing. And although hot Imprezas have become commonplace on our roads, their performance image and reputation for reliability means your WRX should still retain a healthy 60 per cent of its original value after three years.

ABOVE New Impreza is easier on the eye but turbo lag still a problem; we managed 35.2mpg on the open road.

BELOW LEFT Interior won't win any awards but an improvement on old model's.

AUTOCAR VERDICT

It's quicker and cheaper to buy and run. More handsome, too, with its understated looks now reinstated. So the WRX couldn't fail to stride back to the top of the class and wish lists of a nation's car enthusiasts... Could it? That depends on what you want from your performance car. Although better in every area than its predecessor, we're ready for something new now, and the WRX isn't it. No, if you want to reach your destination with adrenal glands pumping healthily, and hands and brow moistened, then the Focus RS will remain your weapon of choice.

That said, as an all-year, all-weather car, the kind that can thrill when asked, yet be content to cosset when the need arises, the Subaru has few peers at this price. For those who also need the practicality of five doors and a big boot, it has none at all.

Still great, no longer greatest   ★★★★

C IS CRACKING

IMPREZA STi SPEC C The mouth-watering, no-compromise spec of the Japanese-market STi Spec C suggests that this is a lightweight special with a heavyweight punch

And just when you thought it was black arm-band time. Just when you thought the game was up. Just as Mitsubishi is putting its Evo lineage in mothballs and the very future of the homologation rally special looks in doubt, Subaru gives us this.

Called STi Spec C, it is nothing more than a throw-the-lot-at-it special designed to shut the traps of anyone insolent enough (yours truly) to assume that the appeal of this type of car is diminishing rapidly. Which surely means that the Spec C is just a Japan-market STi, right, with a few tuning goodies bolted on and a name drafted in from Gran Turismo?

Strictly speaking, yes, it is. But instead of merely a few add-ons, it benefits from pretty much every aftermarket toy that Subaru Technica International can find. And the list of toys available is roughly the size of South London's *Yellow Pages*, leading one to assume that the finished product is somewhat special.

Even forearmed with such knowledge, I always approach these things with caution. Even my geekish ability to remember every different spec of Subaru I've driven is beginning to fail me, and the dank surroundings of a Cheltenham Industrial Estate don't help. But the car does. Sitting outside in solid white

QUICK FACTS

Model	Subaru Impreza STi Spec C
Price	£27,495
On sale	Now
0–62mph	4.2sec (est)
Top speed	150mph (est)
Combined	na
CO$_2$ emissions	na
Weight	1,300kg
Engine Layout	4 cyls opposed, 1,994cc, turbo
Max power	322bhp at 6,500rpm
Max torque	325lb ft at 3,750rpm

NEW CARS

16 APRIL 2003

Volume 236

No 3 | 5532

AUTOCAR
Every week
16 April 2003 £2.10

WE DRIVE THE NEW
MEGA-HATCHES

FUN, AFFORDABLE AND VERY FAST – A NEW POWER GENERATION IS HERE

New Clio V6 250bhp, 0-62 5.8sec, rear drive – surely we're in hot-hatch heaven?

New Peugeot 206 GTi 180
Another legend from the WRC champs?

New Alfa Romeo 147 GTA V6
Alfa sex-bomb v Focus RS and Golf R32

SPEED LIMITS What do you think is safe on the motorway? 80

ABOVE Spec C gets 322bhp and 325lb ft; rear wing now made of carbonfibre.

RIGHT Alloy bonnet helps to save weight; flat-four smoother than ever.

(I've always loved the honesty of white homologators) it cuts a completely different shape on the road. More attractive the 2003 Scooby face may be, but in standard STi spec its stance isn't especially thrusting, and that rear wing is totally over-cooked. Spec C sits 10mm lower, juts its chin a little further forward and its midriff is a mite lower. And it replaces that nasty wing with a spindly carbonfibre thing that couldn't look better if it tried, and one of those manual air-vents in the roof. In my experience, only the most serious Scoobys have a roof vent.

And then there's 322bhp at 6,500rpm and 325lb ft at 3,750rpm, straight out of the box, and a very restrictive exhaust. That's certainly poke aplenty, but factor in a 1,300kg kerb weight, and you've got yourself a ground-attack missile. But, hang on, how the hell has Subaru carved 170kg out of it? Thin glass, lightweight door panels, roof panel, alloy wheels and bonnet for starters. No air con, a pair of DIY windows and no sound deadening for seconds. This is looking like a very trick tool.

It gets better: the engine is radically different. A twin-scroll, big-bearing turbo spins harder, requires less energy and spools earlier than the standard car's. Enlarged induction pipes and a different spec inlet cam working at the commands of a pukka motor sport ECU are now so efficient that the STi exhaust, relatively speaking, has become hopelessly restrictive. Up the pipe diameter and 350bhp can be yours immediately.

We're going to run out of space soon, so I'll stop there. For the full list, dial up www.litchfieldimports. co.uk/subaru/sti japspec.html and digest the most impressively uprated sports car since someone at Porsche decided he fancied the idea of a lightweight 2.7-litre 911 and would name it RS. This is Subaru's RS.

Assessing it away from a circuit is, however, mighty difficult because it is a 110 per cent track weapon. With one very odd concession to everyday refinement: it has the smoothest Subaru flat-four I've ever driven. Equal length manifolds are standard on this car, as they are on all Japanese-spec STis, and the difference is amazing.

The rest is raw aggression: very little ride comfort, intrusive road noise and enough body control to handle any B-road at 290mph. Probably. But the public highway does reveal the one thing you need to know above all else: that the Spec C drives like a Mitsubishi Evo VII. It steers with the same alacrity, loves direction changes and hates understeer.

Even with the restrictive pipes, it's a manically fast car. It pulls hard from 3,500rpm to around 6,800rpm and then gets a little breathless for the final limiter-bound hit. UK-spec Prodrive STis will always be shrinking images in the rear-view mirror, though.

It's at this point that I normally have to bite my tongue and tell you that the £36,000 you need to buy one is fine value when you consider the bits on offer, blah, blah, blah. And you'd rightly throw the mag in the bin at the notion of blowing nearly £40k on an Impreza. However, all this can be yours for just £27,495. On the road, ECU mapped for optimum performance on 95 unleaded, with a year's warranty and Cat 1 alarm all included. Tell me you're not tempted.

As an occasional road car/track car it makes perfect sense. For a young track day fan without the funds for two cars, it would be the perfect vehicle. On tech-value alone, this is the most fascinating Scooby ever. Did I mention the bespoke Bridgestone RE 070 Cup tyres, the new front sub-frame and solid suspension drop links that actually lengthen the wheelbase, or the bigger anti-roll bars? Check out the website, try the car. Like me, you'll be convinced that there's still life in the old homologator.

BELOW Centre binnacle and red back-lit dials unique to Spec C.

POST IMPREZA-NISM

IMPREZA STi TYPE UK Final report: It may fall foul of the PC looks police, but after nine months and 14,500 miles, we are genuinely sorry to see our Impreza STi go

It's the noise I'll miss most. I thought it would be the insane cross-country pace, but it's not; it's the sound it makes. Is there any car currently on sale that has a more melodious idle than the Subaru Impreza STi? After spending six months and 14,500 miles in one, I don't think so.

It's a gutteral, feral sound, best heard on cold starts. With the electronic choke raising the revs, the turbocharged flat four splutters into life and starts clearing its throat at once, leaving an intoxicating growl that never goes away and, all the while, gently fills the cabin with low-frequency thrums. You don't notice this tingling through the steering wheel straight away, but when you do, it's just as pleasing as the induction roar coming from under the bonnet. And now I miss that, too. A lot.

Just to recap, the reason I was getting a daily aural download is that the Scooby was my attempt at running a car that could play the dual role of official *Autocar* track-day tool and vaguely sensible wheels for yours truly.

With fortnightly circuit duty at the Bedford Autodrome, there wasn't any doubt that I'd be tricking it up as much as possible. Sticking to official aftermarket Subaru bits, means getting the Prodrive treatment. So even before taking delivery, we'd opted to push up the £24,995 list price by adding the £1,995 performance pack. Work done on the ECU

WHAT WE LIKE

Amazing cross-country performance, reassurance and talents of four-wheel-drive chassis, seat comfort, reliability, good dealership experiences, the noise it makes

WHAT WE DON'T LIKE

Running costs, disappointing on the track, perceived quality of cabin, lurid decals, huge boot spoiler, ride quality

OUR CARS

14 OCTOBER 2003

Volume 238

No 3 | 5558

ABOVE Subaru takes its place in pit lane for *Autocar* track day; spoiler and lurid decals for instant car park recognition; 17-inch alloys tastefully finished in gold.

I never felt comfortable with having to peer over the bonnet bulge housing the air intake

and exhaust means that power gets nudged up from 262bhp to 300 and torque goes up in tandem, rising from 253lb ft to 299. And, of course, that naughtier exhaust note comes with it.

Barely run in, the STi blasted its way up the M1 to its first *Autocar* track day. Trouble is, when I got there and set about my first exploratory laps of the 2.7-mile South West circuit, I was disappointed. You see, the Subaru, despite the heady promises of its power and chassis, is pretty hard work on the circuit. The problem is that understeer arrives early doors, so rather than adopting a nice, neat apex-clipping style, you need to go in hard, WRC-style, aggressively using the steering and throttle to slide round the problem. It wasn't just my ham-fistedness behind the wheel, either. Hands such as tester-at-large Tiff Needell and touring car driver Phil Bennett agreed with me.

But even though the Scoob occasionally frustrated on the track, it remained a legend for fast road work. It took several thousand miles and an oil change to really loosen up, but when it did, it was fast. Like the exhaust note, second-, third- and fourth-gear acceleration quickly became as addictive as opiates. It simply mashed lesser mortals across country, gobbling up slower-moving traffic with almost arrogant ease. So much so, that I engineered a back-to-back with a 911 Carrera 2, in the interests of science you understand, to see which was quicker. No question, the Subaru won hands down – and that was in the dry. In the wet it would have had an even bigger advantage, such are the liberties I could take.

No surprise, then, that as well as the track-day weapon, the STi was number one choice for *Autocar* staffers about to embark on a B-road blast. No names, no places, but the most dramatic example of the Scoob's cross-country prowess came when *Autocar* staffer X took it on one of his regular, timed, personal B-road challenges. This tortuous 40-mile route encompassing top-end straights, fast sweepers and switchbacks had already been sampled by Mr X in everything from a Maserati Coupé to a 160mph luxury barge, yet the STi shaved an amazing two minutes off his personal best. His verdict? 'Only a 911 Turbo could have gone quicker.'

SUBARU IMPREZA STi vs MITSUBISHI EVO VIII

Our Subaru STi and recently arrived Mitsubishi Evo VIII only overlapped by two weeks. But that's been more than enough time for four *Autocar* staffers to have firm opinions about which one they prefer.

THE CASE FOR THE SCOOBY

This might sound like heresy, but I reckon too many words have been wasted on sorting Scooby from Evo dynamically. Fact is, both will carry you across country faster than anything short of a 911 Turbo, the pace limited only by your talent and fear of the law. It all depends on what def-con level of tuning you indulge in, but the Evo is probably marginally quicker. But who cares, because, like lager v bitter or rugby v football, you're either for one or the other and unlikely to change. And I'm a true blue: for the exhaust note, the chairs, the view down the bonnet to that comedy air scoop, the better ride, refinement and muscularity. But I could do without the daft wing and gold wheels; in fact, about the only thing the Scooby could do to improve its performance would be the addition of an element of surprise.

Ben Oliver

Those of us lucky enough to have driven both these cars in anger tend to have an automatic preference, although a preference for one doesn't automatically preclude the other. If you love the all-round performance of these 4x4 turbo beasts, you can't find the kick anywhere else for the money, so one is a fine substitute for the other. It all comes down to personal taste. That said, if you prefer the Evo, you're an idiot. Some people have no idea what makes a great car great, and they should be flogged to within an inch of their meaningless lives. They fail to recognise the magnificence of Subaru's flat four. Put this sensational motor into a Proton Impian X and it'd instantly be better than the EVO (nearly) because of the way it sounds and goes. That gruff, off-beat grumble is an arresting, urgent thump even at low revs, and as the revs rise and the turbo takes hold, it's freedom, bliss, the greatest moment of your life, in an engine note. The Evo? A tumble dryer.

Bill Thomas

THE CASE FOR THE EVO

When you drive cars this ugly, there have to be compensations. Short of providing ejector seats, these cars couldn't be better equipped for on-road drama. They get closest to mimicking a Playstation steer, but like every electronic driving game, the realism rests heavily on the quality of your faux controls. And it's the same with this pair. The Evo's steering swivels with almost absurdly satisfying precision, yet never has you feeling you're conducting a nervous charge. By contrast, the Impreza's is slower, and fails to rotate with quite the same quality. The gearchange can feel crudely resistant, too, and its body control allows more roll. Despite riding like it had no springs in town, the Evo is more refined. Nit-picking, but at these prices and with such a huge sacrifice of self-image involved, you have the right. So it's the Evo that has the edge, but I'd rather drive it at night.

Richard Bremner

At the risk of sounding like a stuck record, I would like to take this opportunity to clamber once more aboard my soap box and ask WHY? Why do I see a clutch of Impreza WRX STis burbling around London every week, and maybe one Evo – if I'm lucky? Is it purely reputation alone? Has the Scooby cult built up so high that it cannot be toppled? I'm not so sure, particularly now that you hear schoolboys utter the hallowed 'Evo' with even more reverence than was once reserved for 'Impreza'. The noise, then? True, the Subaru's soundtrack is good enough to rival Fat Boy Slim for cult appeal, but then the Lancer doesn't sound too shabby either, and I reckon its sharper looks, fantastic steering, superior performance and super-nimble chassis more than make up for it. So I guess it all comes down to price, because at £24,995 the STi's £2k cheaper than a stock Evo VIII and £4k less than the sublime FQ300.

Alastair Clements

LOGBOOK STi TYPE UK

TEST STARTED 13.02.03

Mileage at start	450
Mileage now	14,458

OPTION

Prodrive performance pack £1,995

PRICES

List price new		£24,995
Total price with options		£26,990
List price now		£24,995
Value now:	Trade	£19,900
	Private	£21,000
	Retail	£22,000

Figures from What Car? Used Car Price Guide

OPTION

Govt urban	18.8mpg
Extra urban	33.2mpg
Combined	25.4mpg
Our test best	26.6mpg
Our test worst	8.3mpg
Our test average	19.4mpg

PERFORMANCE

Max speed	147mph
0–60mph	5.0sec
At 12,000 miles:	
0–30mph	2.0sec
0–40mph	2.5sec
0–50mph	3.5sec
0–60mph	5.0sec
0–70mph	6.6sec
0–80 mph	8.7sec
0–90 mph	10.8sec
0–100mph	12.1sec
30–50mph (4th gear)	3.7sec
50–70mph (5/6th gear)	4.4/8.5sec
Standing qtr mile	13.6sec/100mph
Standing km	25.2sec/129mph

Figures recorded in dry conditions

SERVICING AND TYRES

1,000 miles

Oil & filter changed	£43.00

10,000 miles

Oil & air con filter changed	£295.00

PARTS COSTS EXCLUDING VAT

Oil filter £10.19; air filter £23.24; fuel filter £33.01; front brake pads £170.00; front bumper cover £124.94; rear bumper cover £118.37; alloy wheel £276.96; door mirror £152.26; headlamp £147.06

Repairs Eight new tyres £880, door dents fixed by Dent Devils £75 (01205 751536), new front brake pads £237 (including fitting)

Tyres Bridgestone RE040 225/45 R17 £110 each (excluding VAT) supplied by Micheldever Tyres, 01962 774437

Monthly contract hire rate
£521 on 36-month contract, not exceeding 60,000 miles (HSBC Vehicle Finance, 08459 000888)

COSTS OVER 14,500 MILES

Fuel	£2,695
Oil (non service)	£52
Service costs	£338
Front brake pads (incl fitting)	£237
Eight new tyres	£880
Total running costs	£4,202
Running costs per mile	28.9p
Depreciation	£7,090
Cost per mile (incl depreciation)	77.9p

INSURANCE (GROUP 20)

30-year-old single male, two speeding fines, five years' no-claims bonus, living in high-risk Manchester **£1,851**

35-year-old married male, clean licence, five years' no-claims bonus, living in low-risk Swindon **£886**

All quotes subject to £250 excess from What Car? Insurance (08457 413554)

FINAL VIEW

Brilliant on-road performance, but patchy on the track. Even so, our experience proves that the Subaru STi is as relevant as ever, but you have to live a bad-boy image and huge running costs. Previous reports: 16.04.03; 16.07.03

Back in the real world, though, I never found the STi as user friendly as other Scoobies I've had a close relationship with. Sure, it's as effortless to drive, with no heavy clutch or baulky gearchange giving me grief in the inevitable crosstown traffic jams on the way to work. But I was constantly being reminded that ride quality has suffered in this latest incarnation.

While it's just as beautifully damped as its predecessors, I could never quite fathom why the company's engineers corrupted the ride. Bumps on B-roads that I remember the last car mopping up without a worry, sent jolts through my backside. And worse still, this discomfort carried through on scarred motorway surfaces, making the regular long jaunts more of a chore than they needed to be. Just as well the big-winged Recaro seats are some of the most comfortable in the business.

While I'm in full Victor Meldrew mode, I may as well talk about the costs of ownership. In short, owning an STi meant full commitment from my wallet. Want to get on first-name terms with your local petrol station attendants? Get an Impreza. Even when I was burbling along at A-road speeds, I was lucky to see any fuel returns starting with a two, and doing serious track work saw them plunging to single figures.

Bear in mind, too, that it burns the pricier super-juice and I was adding a tenner's worth of oil every 2,000 miles. Using the Subaru as a track-day toy

took its toll on tyres and brakes, too. More than 14,000 miles of hard contact with the tarmac meant replacing two sets of the 17-inch Bridgestone RE040s, adding the thick end of a grand to the tally. I also needed to bolt on a set of front pads at the 10,000-mile scheduled service: total cost £532 – though the exemplary treatment from my local dealer, Marlborough of Isleworth, in West London, took some of the sting away.

But no amount of slick dealer service ever removed one of the main sticking points I had about Scooby STi ownership – its image. I had reservations at the start of my relationship and, try as hard as I could, I never felt entirely comfortable with that dinner-table-sized spoiler following me around everywhere and having to peer over the huge bonnet bulge housing the air intake. Nor did I really ever appreciate the gold wheels and lurid pink STi decals – pretty hard to avoid as there's one slapped right in the middle of the steering wheel. It's a matter of how other road users treat you, too. BMW-driving Mr Suit-and-Tie and spotty Saxo VTS driver both think

the Scoob's fair game for trafficlight grid starts.

Despite this, the Subaru definitely isn't a motoring irrelevance. Even here at *Autocar* Towers, I've heard mutterings of how Subarishis' days are numbered, left stranded in the '90s by more PC or tasteful tackle.

But my lasting impression of nine months behind the wheel is that anyone who thinks that is well wide of the mark. Evo VIII aside, try thinking of a new car that so successfully combines the ability to serve up such an intense road and track experience, yet can take four adults from London to Edinburgh in comfort and without complaint.

And that's one of the reasons why I really rated (virtually) every mile in mine, and was more than prepared to put up with its lurid looks and arm-and-a-leg running costs. Not as much as I rated the noise it made, though.

ABOVE Understeer makes heavy weather of track work, but on open roads the STi excels, though ride is not as well cushioned as its predecessor's.

As well as a track-day weapon, the STi was our number-one choice for B-road blasts

SWEET AS A NUT

IMPREZA WRX The Impreza Turbo has been updated for the last time, but hatches like the 237bhp Astra VXR are catching up fast. So which is the best £20k nutcase? *By Adam Towler*

So it's still too early to even operate a kettle, and I'm out and into the new Impreza WRX. The featherlight door shuts with a tinny 'clang' and I turn the blocky key in the ignition. There's that familiar rhythmic chirp of the starter motor and the flat four kicks into life with a wobble of the bonnet scoop. It's been a while.

For a few years, the Subaru Impreza seemed the essential motoring purchase. In 1995, the Impreza started to look tasty and we woke up to a performance bargain that could trounce just about anything on the road. Remember the Series McRae? It was dark blue, had gold wheels and went 'worba-worba' with that deep guttural engine note. I really, really wanted one.

But eventually things changed. The Impreza Mk2 arrived five years ago to gasps of horror at its bug-eyed looks and awkward proportions. It was nicer inside, more refined and able in the corners, but heavier, slower and somehow less alive. Subaru UK also brought in the even madder STi models and Imprezas became all about big wings and power in a bitter struggle to outdo the Mitsubishi Evo. The standard WRX seemed less dramatic. However, now there's a new WRX with a designer nose, chassis revisions and, crucially, a new 2.5-litre engine. We can't wait to find out if the magic is back.

In the Impreza's rear-view mirror is something very much from the present: the current hot hatch bad-boy, the Vauxhall Astra VXR. Looking as angry as ever in bright red, the Astra represents where the market has gone. Where once the Impreza stood alone as a performance bargain, it's now surrounded by a new kind of hot hatch that costs around 20 grand and packs a minimum of 200 turbocharged horses.

AGEING DISGRACEFULLY

It doesn't take long for some rather painful home truths to emerge about the Impreza, however. This is now an old car, and feels as such. The interior plastics are cheap and mostly hard to the touch, and the overall design is simply crude. We might have classed this interior as an improvement over the old car's five years ago, but we weren't blind to its failings then, and standards elsewhere have risen greatly during the intervening years. The seat won't drop low enough for me nor push far enough back, and the electric sunroof robs much-needed headroom. I have to drop the backrest to fit in, which removes all the supportive qualities of the leather sports seats.

The roar of the M4's asphalt is soon drumming through the wheelarches and making its nagging presence felt, as is the gushing of the wind and the noise of the suspension. To be honest, the shortage of refinement is a shock. Turn up the stereo to drown it out and each thump of the bass line sends the speakers and surrounding trim into a nervous zizz. On a £20,000 car that's not good enough. There's a long way to go and I'm fed up of cruising already. Time to turn off the motorway and take the scenic route, and time to swap cars, too.

The Astra couldn't be more different if it tried. Of course, it's a hatchback for starters. Inside it's very dark, thanks to the unremitting blackness of the interior and the limited glass area of the three-door Astra bodyshell. Plenty of people find it claustrophobic, but I like it. There's something reassuring about its cosy confines, the shallow screen and letterbox rear glass. The Recaro seats look extreme – as if they could support the Red Arrows during a high-g turn – but the slightly odd

> 'THE SUBARU PROVIDES REAL, THREE-DIMENSIONAL DRIVING COMPARED TO THE ASTRA'S POINT AND SQUIRT'

FEATURE

11 OCTOBER 2005

Volume 246

No 2 | 5660

ergonomics and diving front roof section mean I'll still be desperately fiddling with the seat adjustments when we return to London tonight. But the VXR is truly dominated by only one thing: the turbo. As soon as you even contemplate acceleration there's the familiar VXR 'hawww', so loud it's impossible not to smirk.

As we up the pace and forge deeper into the countryside, it soon becomes clear that there's little to choose between them in outright performance – even if they achieve it in very different ways. Without the Sport button pressed, the VXR's throttle is lazier than a hung-over teenager; push it and the car becomes as hyperactive as said teen after 10 cans of Red Bull. It isn't actually that laggy, but there is very little action until the sudden violent rush of boost as 237bhp and 236lb ft of torque seem to arrive instantaneously. The big flaw of this car, however, is the throttle's inability to offer the driver any real control of what goes on under that arched bonnet. Put simply, it doesn't seem to matter whether you open the throttle five per cent or 80 per cent: you always get 100 per cent.

The Impreza feels much more progressive. With the new 2.5-litre engine, power is up 5bhp to 227bhp and torque swells to 236lb ft from 221lb ft, with a useful increase in the mid-range. There's a sensation of the turbo spinning up at low revs before it thrusts you along the road with a more elastic shove than the rabid VXR. Like all Subarus, it thrives on being revved and, should you rev it, it's plenty quick. Despite a new electronic throttle it always responds in a predictable and linear fashion.

However – and I'm distraught about this – it doesn't make that noise any more. New, equal-length exhaust manifolds rob the flat four of its voice. They might be more environmentally efficient, but rarely has progress been more painful.

The inevitable fuel stop for cars and drivers is also a chance to compare the looks of our two challengers side by side. I will be blunt about the Subaru, although it gives me no pleasure to be so, because visual appeal is a core element of these cars. Shorn of STi battledress, this is a visually undesirable car. The new corporate nose, featuring the 'spread wings grille and hawk-eye headlamps', has been plastered onto an awkward, ageing and upright saloon with predictable results. On its own, the new nose isn't bad, but it doesn't turn the Impreza into a dynamic design overnight. It's the details that really grate, such as the new Lexus-style rear lights of the sort boy racers love to fit to their tweaked Citroën Saxos. Is this what buyers who can afford a £20,900 car – and its huge running costs – really want?

The VXR has no such worries. It owns aggression in hatch form. The 18-inch alloys fill every last sliver of space under the arches and the VXR body armour makes the already handsome Astra Sport Hatch heroically chunky and macho. The message is clear: this is a fast car, plain and simple. Some of the details, such as the chrome headlight and foglight surrounds, and the naff side repeaters, will already have prospective VW Golf GTi owners sneering, but deep down I'm genetically programmed to respond to this shape.

ABOVE Impreza's new nose isn't the prettiest – we've obscured it here for your benefit.

LEFT Subaru's new rear lights are a bit naff, while the Astra looks bang up to date.

OPPOSITE Impreza badly needs more seating adjustment and better quality.

BRUTAL DRIVE

The VXR drives a lot how it looks. It's a brutal experience that demands you master the car quickly and lead it at all times. Thankfully, today is dry, otherwise we might as well have turned around and driven straight home, such would have been the Subaru's advantage. On these clear, sweeping mountain roads the VXR experience is like this: Bang! Boost, squirm, turbo noise, wrists called into action – must keep car pointing straight. Down the road. Wham! Hard on the brakes, turn in – nose streaks for the apex – rear edges out, car virtually drifts through. More boost, whoosh, more squirming, then hard on the brakes, turn in left, then right, the car pivoting directly beneath you rather than around the nose. It's brutal, and not especially pretty, but it can be very fast.

IMPREZA WRX vs ASTRA VXR

MAKE	SUBARU	VAUXHALL
Model	**IMPREZA WRX**	**ASTRA VXR**
Price	£20,900	£18,995
On sale in UK	Now	Now
0–60mph	5.4sec (claimed)	6.4sec
0–100mph	na	16.4sec
Top speed	143mph (claimed)	143mph
Power	227bhp at 5,600rpm	237bhp at 5,600rpm
Torque	236lb ft at 3,600rpm	236lb ft at 2,400rpm
Power to weight	161bhp per tonne	170bhp per tonne
Emissions (CO_2)	244g/km	223g/km
On this test	19.1mpg	20.4mpg
Urban/combined	19.6/27.4mpg	21.6/30.4mpg
Real-world range	252 miles	233 miles
Length/width	4,465/1,990mm	4,290/2,033mm
Height/wheelbase	1,440/2,525mm	1,092/2,616mm
Track (front/rear)	1,485/1,480mm	1,420/1,410mm
Weight	1,410kg	1,393kg
Fuel tank	60 litres	52 litres
Boot (max)	349 litres	302 litres
Engine layout	Flat four, 2,457cc, turbo	4 cyls in line, 1,998cc, turbo
Installation	Front, longitudinal, four-wheel drive	Front, transverse, front-wheel drive
Specific output	92bhp per litre	119bhp per litre
Bore/stroke	99.5/79.0mm	86.0/86.0
Gearbox type	5-speed manual	6-speed manual
Ratios/mph per 1,000rpm	1st 3.45/5.2 2nd 1.95/9.1 3rd 1.37/13.0 4th 0.97/18.3 5th 0.74/24.1	1st 3.82/5.1 2nd 2.05/9.5 3rd 1.30/15.0 4th 0.96/20.3 5th 0.74/26.3 6th 0.61/31.9
Front suspension	MacPherson struts, coil springs, anti-roll bar	MacPherson struts, coil springs, anti-roll bar
Rear suspension	MacPherson struts, coil springs, anti-roll bar	Torsion beam coil springs
Front brakes	294mm ventilated discs	321mm ventilated discs
Rear brakes	266mm ventilated discs	278mm ventilated discs
Wheels front/rear	17-inch alloy	18-inch alloy
Tyres front/rear	215/45 R17	225/40 R18

The Astra is less happy when the road tightens, and you need to summon all your patience if you're not to get untidy through slower corners. Without a limited-slip differential, it'll light up the inside front tyre around a hairpin and leave a thick black line and a cloud of tyre smoke. So sharp is the steering that it's very hard to be progressive with the VXR, and difficult to get a decent flow going – especially when the brakes are annoyingly soft and unprogressive in their operation, if effective. Add in a bumpy section of road on the exit of a corner and you've got a recipe for a busy drive.

The Subaru requires a totally different approach. It needs a much calmer, steadier hand. The steering is much more linear, like the throttle, and possesses more feel. You guide it through corners and delicately pick your line, free from having to manage the effects of all that torque passing purely through the front wheels. Naturally it has outstanding traction: you can give it full throttle amazingly early in a hairpin and feel every last pony power into the road as you're flung forwards.

The VXR can't keep up. The Subaru's narrower tyres generate less actual grip than the VXR's, and the suspension is also initially softer, although the

rebound damping is quite severe, which gives it a typically Subaru nodding-head effect over bumpy stretches. Throw it at a sequence of corners and it rolls more than the Astra, although the WRX's actual pace is on a different level.

But the Impreza is only just getting warmed up. Lift off the throttle and turn into a corner sharply and the rear of the car will step out benignly: time it right and the nose will be locked onto the apex. Now you can give it full throttle and drift through the corner without a trace of understeer. Link all these elements together and the Subaru dances on a demanding road. It's talking a language the Astra could never hope to understand: Keats next to the VXR's monosyllabic grunting; real, three-dimensional driving compared to the Astra's point and squirt.

DECISION TIME

It is very late, very dark and I think we might be lost. So I pull rank and get myself into the VXR for the return journey. My eardrums are hurting from the Subaru's tinny stereo and I crave the Astra's extra refinement, comfort and modernity. Whether they are enough to make the Vauxhall a good ownership proposition I'm not so sure. But then whether I could spend £20,900 on this Impreza and not find myself at the local Golf GTi emporium with my own cash is another hard question. The Impreza is both as bad and as fantastic as ever from behind the wheel, but please, Subaru, it really is time for some new wrapping.

ABOVE Show the Impreza a bumpy, twisty road and it comes alive.

OPPOSITE Impreza's new 2.5 pumps out 227bhp next to 2.0 VXR's 237bhp.

Subaru's progressive power delivery outgunned by Astra's turbo hit.

SUBARU IMPREZA STi

IMPREZA STi TYPE UK It has a new face, but this is not just a facelifted Impreza: with a new engine, revised chassis and tweaked transmission it's a whole new Scooby. Is it still great to drive?

The easiest way to greet the 'all new, massively more powerful and dynamically facelifted' Subaru Impreza STi is with your tongue firmly in the side of your cheek. Because let's face it, on the surface the 'all new, massively improved' £26,400 Impreza STi looks an awful lot like old Impreza STi, only this time sporting a dubious new nose job and... that's about it.

If that were genuinely the case, however, we wouldn't be wasting your time here with yet another road test of yet another hot Impreza. In reality, and despite appearing remarkably similar to its predecessor, this time Subaru really has gone to town on the STi. Not only is there a brand new 2.5-litre engine in place of the previous model's 2.0-litre turbocharged four, but everything from the suspension to the gearbox and even the legendary all-wheel-drive system has either been modified or replaced. The result, says Subaru, is the fastest, most agile Impreza ever to go on sale in the UK, and that includes the limited-edition 22B that tore up our streets at the end of the last century.

So, apart from the take-it-or-leave-it new nose and slightly smaller bonnet scoop, what else is new for the 2006 STi? Let's start at the front. The engine is totally different and is now 2,457cc, half a litre bigger than before. It's still a turbocharged four-cylinder boxer, but with the extra capacity comes

QUICK FACTS

Model	STi Type UK
Price	£26,400
On sale	Now
0–60mph	5.1sec
Top speed	158mph
70–0mph	46.5m
Skidpan	0.97g
Economy	23.6mpg
CO_2 emissions	257g/km

ROAD TEST

6 DECEMBER 2005

Volume 244
No 10 | 5668

ROAD TEST STi TYPE UK

ACCELERATION

	1.5s	2.7s	3.7s	5.1s	6.5s	8.1s	10.4s	12.6s	15.9s	20.0s	25.3s
30mph	40	50	60	70	80	90	100	110	120		130

0 — 5s — 10s — 15s — 20s — 25s

Standing qtr mile 13.5sec/103.5mph **Standing km** 24.9sec/129.6mph **30–70mph** 5.0sec

BRAKING

	8.5m	23.5m	46.5m
30mph-0		50mph-0	70mph-0

0 — 10m — 20m — 30m — 40m

60–0mph 2.7sec   **Indicated mph at 30/70** 32/75mph

MAXIMUM SPEEDS

6th 152mph/5,650rpm **5th** 150/7,200
4th 121/7,200   **3rd** 90/7,200
2nd 61/7,200   **1st** 38/7,200

ACCELERATION IN GEAR

MPH	6th	5th	4th	3rd	2nd
20–40	14.4	9.4	7.2	4.1	2.1
30–50	13.6	8.2	4.9	3.0	1.8
40–60	11.2	6.8	3.8	2.5	
50–70	9.7	5.5	3.4	2.6	
60–80	8.6	5.0	3.5	2.9	
70–90	8.3	5.1	3.7		
80–100	8.0	5.3	4.2		
90–110	8.5	5.8	5.2		
100–120		6.8			

HANDLING

Lateral acceleration	0.97g
Balance	Understeer
Seat support	Excellent

NOISE

Idle/max revs in 3rd 49/79dbA
30/50/70mph 69/72/74dbA

FUEL CONSUMPTION

Test	Average	23.6mpg
	Touring	28.5mpg
	Track	7.3mpg
Claimed	Urban	18.5mpg
	Extra-urban	34.0mpg
	Combined	25.9mpg
Tank capacity	60 litres	
Test range	300 miles	

HEADLIGHTS

Dipped beam Good
Full beam Very good
Test notes Good range and spread

TESTER'S NOTES

We are baffled by this car's awful ride. What's happened to Subaru's ability to tune springs and dampers to a point where its cars would flow smoothly across the ground instead of thump into it? Not convinced by the new corporate nose, either, though that's more of a matter of opinion than judgement.

notably more thump low down plus a wee bit more power. The headline figures are 276bhp at 6,000rpm and 289lb ft at 4,000rpm; 16bhp and 36lb ft more than before, both achieved at slightly lower revs.

The six-speed 'box has been revised to provide longer ratios and more relaxed running where it matters, namely in fourth, fifth and sixth. It also has a sharper shift action, says Subaru, thanks to carbon-plated synchros on four, five and six.

On top of this, the system that allows a driver manually to alter the amount of torque that flows to the front and rear differentials has been honed. In normal driving the split is 41:59 front to rear, but this can be altered by playing with the dial next to the handbrake to make the STi almost 100 per cent rear-drive in momentary bursts.

The diffs themselves have also been uprated to provide greater stability on rough surfaces, sharper turn-in response and, best of all, much more control of the rear end when you come off the throttle mid-corner. Gone, says Subaru, are the days when you could throw your Impreza sideways into a bend by backing off the throttle; now the car will sort the

Little has changed in the cabin – it's still more functional than aesthetically pleasing; six-speed gearbox good to use.

slide out largely on its own, which is perhaps 90 per cent a good thing and 10 per cent a pity.

The suspension, steering and brakes are largely the same as before, albeit with minor modifications to improve performance. The rack and pinion steering, for example, has a new damper specifically designed to reduce kickback over rough surfaces. The tyres are a big step forward. All STis come fitted with a new type of Bridgestone, the RE070, which is effectively a semi-cut slick with tread. When warm this tyre should provide heart-stopping levels of grip in the dry – but, says Bridgestone, unlike many other cup tyres it works just as well in the wet, too.

Inside, the STi gets a new steering wheel and gearlever, even beefier seats and a fresh set of instruments that highlight the car's motorsport heritage, as if you were ever in any doubt. Of more significance, arguably, is the fact that there are now side airbags and a Category One alarm with satellite tracking as standard.

On the move, the first thing you notice about the new STi is the ride quality, which is frankly the wrong side of dreadful. There was a time when Imprezas

would glide across rough surfaces in a manner similar to a Lotus Elise. Not any more. Which is a pity, because at a stroke this foible seriously limits the car's appeal badly and will eradicate it from many potential owners' wish lists.

Once you've accepted that comfort plays little part in the STi's dynamic repertoire it is a stunning machine to drive, though not one that's as good to listen to as its more charismatic predecessor. No

OPPOSITE Refreshed dials smart, easy to read; 2.5-litre engine is more powerful and more frugal than old 2.0-litre one.

WHAT IT COSTS

IMPREZA STi TYPE UK		EQUIPMENT CHECKLIST	
On-the-road price	£26,995	Prodrive spring kit	£225
Price as tested	£26,995	Bluetooth hands-free kit	£225
Retained value 3yrs	na	Sat-nav CD tuner	£699
Typical PCP pcm	na	Parking sensors	£165
Contract hire pcm	£493	Rain sensing wipers	£195
Cost per mile	63.7p	Front fog lamps	£235
CO_2	257g/km		
Tax at 22/40% pcm	£172/312		
Insurance	20	■ = Standard na = not available	

SPECIFICATIONS STi TYPE UK

DIMENSIONS

Front track 1,490mm Rear track 1,495mm Width (inc mirrors) 1,940m
Front interior width 1,410mm

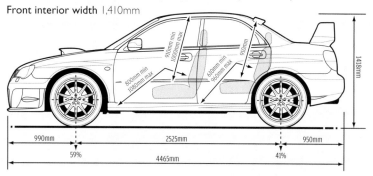

ENGINE

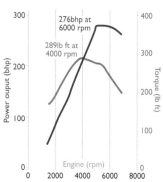

276bhp at 6000 rpm
289lb ft at 4000 rpm

Type	4 cyls, boxer, 2,457cc
Made of	Alloy head & block
Installation	Front, longitudinal
Power	276bhp at 6,000rpm
Torque	289lb ft at 4,000rpm
Red line	7,200rpm
Power to weight	185bhp per tonne
Torque to weight	193lb ft per tonne
Specific output	112bhp per litre
Bore/stroke	87.5/94.0mm
Compression ratio	8.0:1
Valve gear	4 per cyl, dohc
Fuel type	Petrol

TRANSMISSION

Type	Four-wheel drive
Gearbox	6-speed manual

Ratios/mph per 1,000rpm
Final drive ratio 3.9

1st 3.63/5.2	2nd 2.23/8.5
3rd 1.52/12.5	4th 1.14/16.7
5th 0.89/21.4	6th 0.71/26.9

CHASSIS AND BODY

Construction	Steel unibody
Weight	1,495kg
Weight as tested	1,493kg
Drag coefficient	0.33
Wheels	8J × 17in
Made of	Alloy
Tyres	225/45ZR17
Spare	Space saver

STEERING

Type Hydraulically assisted rack and pinion
Turns lock-to-lock 2.6
Turning circle 11.6m

SUSPENSION

Front MacPherson struts, coil springs, anti-roll bars
Rear Independent, coil springs, anti-roll bars

BRAKES

Front 330mm ventilated discs
Rear 305mm ventilated discs
Anti-lock Yes
Parking brake Hand operated

SAFETY

Twin front and side airbags, anti-lock brakes

matter: the new engine may not sound as exciting as the old one but in every other way it moves the game on. Low down, especially, it's now seriously responsive, so even if you put your foot down at 2,000rpm in fifth the pick up is almost instant and the acceleration suitably strong.

As ever, though, it's only when you take the car by the scruff and metaphorically throw it down the road that the most appealing side of the STi's character reveals itself. It's not everyone's cup of tea, but the fact remains there are few cars on this earth that can stay with a well-driven Impreza STi – and the new car is quantifiably faster than any production Impreza that's gone before.

Statistically it's only a small bit quicker than the previous model; 0–60mph takes 5.1sec, 0–100mph 12.6sec and the standing quarter mile 13.5sec, each slight improvements. But on the road the combined might of the extra mid-range go and the monumentally grippy tyres mean the new STi would leave the old one for dust over a winding B-road. Considering how rapid the old car was, that really is some achievement.

For a lot of the time it was raining when we tested the STi and we can vouch for the extra

Few tweaks at rear; front gets new grille and lights and smaller air scoop.

wet-road grip offered by those new Bridgestones. At the same time, however, the extra stiffness of the suspension and the way the diffs are now set up means there is more understeer on a greasy road. Just occasionally it feels as if it wants to go straight on and there's nothing you can do to stop it other than shed speed, rapidly. Which, it must be said, is a task the big Brembo brakes dismiss with ease and without so much as a trace of fade.

Anyone familiar with the workmanlike but hardly sumptuous interior of previous Imprezas will feel at home in the new cabin. Although there are one or two nice touches such as the illuminated STi logo and a marginally more attractive set of instruments, it's business as usual inside. Same goes for the rear seats and boot, which offer fine accommodation for adults and their luggage.

Living with an STi day-to-day has never been that simple, and in this context the super-stiff ride does it no favours. Nor does a test combined fuel consumption of just 23.6mpg, although this is a small improvement over the previous model's economy. It also produces marginally less CO_2 than the old car, but not enough to make it any less expensive to insure (it's in group 20) or to run in terms of company car tax.

AUTOCAR VERDICT

In many ways the new STi is better, faster and more exciting than its predecessor. And if the raison d'être of a machine like this is to carry you down the road as rapidly as possible, then it achieves its aims with devastating precision. But surely Subaru could have fitted slightly softer suspension while also allowing it to hit its dynamic targets? In the event it didn't, and the STi is very much an acquired taste as a result. Even so, when the mood takes you it's one heck of a fine fast car.

Not quite the rule-breaker it once was

IMPREZA WRX

IMPREZA WRX 5-DOOR Rory Lumsdon enjoyed his Impreza WRX's blend of four-wheel drive, turbo grunt and practicality, especially after a sneaky visit to Prodrive

Left three, 200 over crest, right one, 500, right four, 200 caution school, 50 hairpin left, 50 yump, 50 yump, left six into office car park.

Now that's what I call commuting. Don't worry, on my way to work I didn't really race along like Petter Solberg on the Monte Carlo. Not often, anyway. But that didn't stop me dreaming.

Even now that the Impreza's gone, the dreaming continues. I look at demanding stretches of road and think, "That'd be great in the WRX." It's especially true in winter. On a mud and crud-strewn British B-road, an Impreza's combination of pace and agility make it near-unbeatable. Rain? Bring it on. Fog? Forget about it. Snow? So what?

Come to think of it, the Impreza's not bad on a dry road in the sunshine either. But after 12 months and almost 15,000 miles, it's not the WRX's pace that has left the biggest impression; it's the fact that the worse the weather gets, the faster the Subaru goes.

At least that's how it seems, because everyone else is hamstrung by an ability to get power to the road. In bad conditions, you don't need a 4x4 if you really want to make progress, but you do need all-wheel drive. Chris Harris made that very point to me last winter, when he was spending much of his time going sideways in a Merc C55 AMG estate.

At the time, Harris reckoned a WRX wagon was what he needed. Now, of course, he's got an Audi RS4 wagon, which is about as practical as the Impreza, and as grippy. But while it's quicker and much more upmarket, it's also wider and heavier, costs roughly double what the WRX does to buy, and a whole heap more to run.

Not that an Impreza WRX is cheap in everyday use, mind you. Our car started off as a standard £22,900 WRX SL (though I've seen dealers selling

them for at least £3,000 less). SL specification means it comes with leather seats (heated up front) and a sunroof, and costs an extra £1,500. I was happy to have the sunroof, and the leather meant the seats are easy to wipe clean.

Straight out of the box, the WRX has 227bhp and 237lb ft. That's sufficient to propel it from 0–60mph in 6.1sec. In fact, the standard WRX is pretty good all round, but we were disappointed by the diminished thrum from the new, bigger 2.5-litre flat four. The old 2.0-litre engine emitted a more distinctive sound, and we feel its loss is a bad thing that the new engine's improved torque doesn't really make up for.

The handling, however, is as good as ever. Jump from a WRX to any of the current crop of hot hatches and you'll wonder what happened. None of them – much-praised Focus ST included – get anywhere close to offering the involvement of the WRX. The steering in particular is fabulous; there's a world of feedback, oodles of feel and no torque steer.

The controls are great too. All the pedals are perfectly placed (heel-and-toe changes are a cinch), and the five-speed gearbox is clunky but satisfying, if reluctant to go into reverse. The driving position is also spot on, with plenty of adjustability for drivers short or tall, slimline or full fat. But every modern hatch offers a much more pleasant cabin than the Impreza. It feels plasticky and dated, from the very 1980s green LED clock (as still used by Lexus, in fairness) to the Dixons-special stereo, the quality of sound from which isn't up to much.

Then there's the ride. Next to an Astra VXR, the Impreza is quite compliant and well damped, but on motorways it has a tendency to bob up and down like a nodding dog's head. The nodding seems to disappear above 90mph, but by then so could your

'TO MY MIND, WHETHER OR NOT YOU BUY AN IMPREZA
WRX REALLY DEPENDS ON WHERE YOU LIVE.'

OUR CARS

21 FEBRUARY 2007

Volume 251

No 8 | 5729

ABOVE Scooby was unruffled by wet roads, fog or even snow. Lowering the suspension and bolting on OZ wheels even made it look vaguely handsome.

licence. After one especially motorway-bound day, covering nearly 500 miles, I had serious sense of humour failure. There were only two options: stop using motorways, or increase the car's power, lower it and fit bigger wheels.

Naturally we went for the latter. It's not quite as mad a scheme as it might initially seem, either. Yes, the total cost including fitting is around £4,000, but you get a totally transformed car. In fact, I'd say you get a car that's better than the £26,995 (saloon-only) STi. Power goes up to 266bhp, torque to 310lb ft, and 0–60mph drops to 5.3sec. In-gear times are cut

too; 30–70mph goes down from 6.0sec to 5.3sec. And if the car's now-insane rapidity doesn't impress you, the sound from the bigger-bore exhaust certainly will. With the stainless steel Prodrive exhaust on, the Impreza rumbles like not-so-distant thunder.

You don't have to get bigger wheels and shorter springs with the engine upgrade, but we were enticed by some lovely 10-spoke, 18-inch OZ numbers, so we thought we might as well get the springs too. Suddenly the whole car looked more purposeful, and amazingly its ride improved as well.

To check whether or not the motorway ride was

SUBARU IMPREZA WRX   BAD

RUBBISH RADIO
Sound quality (even from CDs) is mediocre. And it's got a cassette deck, which is as much use as an eight-track.

AFTERMARKET-STYLE LIGHTS
The WRX isn't the world's biggest sophisticate, but these lights would be more at home on a souped-up Saxo.

POOR PLASTICS
The Impreza is remarkably robust. But you'd never know from looking at or touching the cheap-feeling dash.

PRACTICALLY THRILLING
It's more hatch than estate, but the Impreza still blends load-lugging ability with track-day agility like few others.

any better, we headed up the M1 to an *Autocar* track day at Bedford Autodrome. It was, but there was still a tendency to jiggle. Pleasingly, however, there was also a tendency to perform big powerslides on the track, especially in the wet.

Such behaviour won't help your tyres, but then as we've already said, running costs are high. After an initial oil service at 1,000 miles (free labour, not parts), you need to get the car serviced every 8,000 miles. We just escaped the second service, but you can expect to get on first-name terms with your dealer. Fortunately for us, that was the excellent Bell & Colvill in West Horsley, Surrey.

So would I recommend you buy an Impreza WRX? Probably. It isn't cheap to run, especially as it only really likes posh petrol. But then again it did manage a reasonable 23.7mpg overall, including lots of city driving, some track work and plenty of heavy right feet. It's also likely to be reliable (Subaru regularly nudges the top 10 in the *What Car?* reliability survey), so you can count on it being faithful, too.

But to my mind, whether or not you buy an Impreza WRX really depends on where you live. If you live in the sticks, with lovely twisty roads, I can't recommend it highly enough. But if you reside in the city, or spend most of your time on motorways, the Impreza's poor refinement is a high price to pay in return for the few opportunities you'll get to exploit its considerable talents. It's still every bit as good to drive as it was in 2001, but unfortunately it's no more refined.

So should you wait for the new Impreza that's due to be unveiled at the New York Motor Show in April? I wouldn't. It will no doubt be more refined, but there are no plans for either an estate or a WRX version. And I reckon that means they're getting rid of the best Impreza of the lot.

LOGBOOK IMPREZA WRX

TEST STARTED 22.12.05

| Mileage at start | 147 |
| Mileage now | 14,690 |

PRICES

List price then	£22,900
List price now	£22,945
Price as tested	£26,900
Value now: Trade	£14,325/£15,825
Private	£15,500/£17,000
Retail	£16,325/£18,000

OPTION

Prodrive Performance Pack £1,700
Prodrive springs £225
18-inch WRC-1 wheels with Pirelli P Zero Nero tyres £1,599.96
All plus fitting of circa £400. Added at 8,500miles

FUEL CONSUMPTION

Official combined	27.4mpg
Test average	23.7mpg
Test best	28.9mpg
Test worst	14.2mpg
Fuel tank	60 litres
Real-world range	220 miles

PERFORMANCE

	Pre-PPP	Post-PPP
Top speed	143mph	144mph
0–60mph	6.1sec	5.3sec
0–100mph	16.0sec	14.4sec
30–70mph	6.0sec	5.3sec

ENGINE

4 cyl, 2457cc, turbocharged, petrol, front, longitudinal, 4wd
Power (before) 227bhp at 5,600rpm
Torque (before) 237lb ft at 3,600rpm
Power (after) 266bhp at 5,700rpm
Torque (after) 310lb ft at 3,000rpm

WHEELS/TYRES (BEFORE)

17in alloy, 215/45 R17
Bridgestone Potenza RE050

WHEELS/TYRES (AFTER)

18in alloy, 225/40 R18
Pirelli P Zero Nero

SERVICE/RUNNING COSTS

Contract hire rate	na
CO_2 output	244g/km
Company car tax rate	30 per cent
1,000-mile service	£60.21
Total Service costs	£414.32
Fuel costs (2,790 litres, 98RON)	£2,735
Running costs incl. fuel	£3,149.32
Running cost per mile	22p
Depreciation	£7,400/9,000
Cost per mile (inc depreciation, pre-/post-PPP upgrade)	73p/84p
Faults	none

DEPRECIATION

Hard to accurately gauge due to the PPP pack. Keep it longer and it's better.

BETTER

STEERING
Wheely good. Better than the Impreza STi's by a mile and provides plenty of feel during B-road antics.

ENGINE
A corker. Beautifully linear power delivery and all the character you could ask for, especially post-Prodrive.

BONNET SCOOP
The Impreza's far from beautiful, but I love that bonnet scoop, even when removing dead birds from it (not really).

BEST

CHASSIS AND 4WD
Whatever the road (or track, or field), whatever the weather, the WRX is reliably thrilling and dependably fast.

SUBARU IMPREZA S-GT

This Japanese version of the latest Impreza provides the best indication yet of how the 'official' WRX STi will feel: great

Forget the guff put about by Subaru suggesting the new Impreza is now fully into mainstream motoring, that it's now very much a normal car first and a performance car second. This is the new WRX STi (sort of) and it restores the status quo of Impreza-ness.

'Sort of an STi' because this a Japanese version of it, dubbed the S-GT to differentiate it from the old model, for which it's intended to be a more grown-up replacement.

The S-GT is available through Litchfield Imports now and has a few differences – not bad ones – from official UK WRXs. Its suspension is in Japanese spec (all officially exported WRXs will have slightly softer suspension), and rather than the 2.5-litre, single-scroll turbocharged flat four that will be fitted to UK-spec cars (see panel), the S-GT is powered by a twin-scroll 2.0-litre engine. The ECU is tweaked by Litchfield to make a healthy 306bhp and meet Euro4 emissions regulations. The 2.5-litre unit can't do both so easily, and not at all while revving to 7,500rpm.

The car we've driven is the Litchfield development car and its throttle mapping hasn't been finalised, but even so it's pretty good; there's bags of torque, just a little lag and it pulls strongly right past 7,000rpm.

This version even looks okay – compared with

SO GOOD

- Entertaining handling, once you get used to body roll.
- Far better ride than before.
- Engine is a real belter.
- Decent room for adults and their luggage.

NO GOOD

- It still doesn't look great, despite performance styling add-ons.
- Only a five-speed gearbox; it needs six ratios.
- Official WRX STi is now coming here after all.

FIRST DRIVE

10 OCTOBER 2007

Volume 254

No 2 | 5762

FACTFILE

Model	Subaru Impreza Litchfield S-GT Sport
Price	£22,995
On sale	Now
Top speed	157mph (limited)
0–62mph	5.0sec
Economy	na
CO_2	"Less than 225g/km"
Kerb weight	1,395kg
Engine	4 cyls, horizontally opposed, 1,994cc, turbo, petrol
Installation	Front, transverse, 4wd
Power	306bhp at 6,800rpm
Torque	315lb ft at 3,000rpm
Gearbox	5-spd manual
Fuel tank	64 litres
Boot	538 litres
Wheels	18in, alloy

NEW TECH – POWER GAMES

Japanese-market hot Imprezas get a 2.0-litre engine with variable intake and exhaust valve timing and a twin-scroll turbo, instead of the single-scroll 2.5-litre engine that UK cars will get. Unique to the 2.0-litre engine is an 'eco' mode that changes the ECU mapping to allow the car to run more economically and with reduced power. Litchfield's mapping will be type approved to Euro4 standards. With eco mode on, it will come in at under 225g/km of CO_2 and should offer 15 per cent better economy. It has the same functionality as 'SI Drive', recently introduced on the 3.0-litre Legacy and Outback.

cooking Imprezas, at least. The grille is meaner, the wheels are wider and Litchfield will eventually increase the track to fill the arches properly when it finalises its 'Sport' suspension settings.

But even on the regular S-GT springs and dampers, it's not half bad. The ride is massively better than the old Impreza's (bushes and anti-roll bars are soft as standard) while the steering is accurate and nicely weighted. It feels more sophisticated than the previous car.

It still corners fast, too, albeit strangely; the phrase "to slingshot out of bends", formerly only the preserve of rubbish advertising copywriters, is strangely apt here.

When the Impreza corners hard, its tyres squeal, there's quite a lot of lean and lateral acceleration increases until it thinks about understeering for, ooh, about half a second. Then power apportions itself to the back through a limited-slip rear diff, and with a bit of dive at the rear and an inch of lateral slip, it bounces itself out of its cornering stance and into a straight-line one. It's very effective and, once you're used to it, a lot of fun.

And that's also the most encouraging thing about this car; in this raw, undeveloped flavour the new Impreza is already fast and entertaining.

And think about what we've still got to come: the STi, a Litchfield Type 25, Prodrive versions and countless special editions. If this is the Impreza going mainstream, bring it on.

FIRST VERDICT ★★★★
**Don't believe the anti-hype:
the hot Impreza is not dead after all**

OPPOSITE Body roll? You bet. But just when you think all hope is lost, the S-GT picks up its tail and scurries out of corners.

LEFT Eco mode boosts mpg by 15 per cent.

BELOW S-GT is very different from previous extreme Imprezas to drive, but it bodes well for future development.

CHARM OFFENSIVE

IMPREZA WRX STi Forget the base model; the new WRX STi is where the new Impreza should really shine. It does, says Hilton Holloway after flat-out laps of Fuji

The last – and first – time I was at Fuji Speedway was in October 2005. This extraordinary place stuck in my mind for a number of reasons, not least the awesome sound of the Lexus LF-A V10 supercar on a demonstration drive down the mile-long main straight.

High in the hills and under the shadow of Mount Fuji (and often in the grip of extreme rain and mist) this 2.8-mile circuit had just been completely rebuilt and redeveloped in what was eventually a successful bid to regain the Japanese Grand Prix.

It had a spooky quality, so eerily clean and tidy was it. Concrete walls were a perfectly matt, mottled grey and the floors of the pit garages spotless in shiny grey resin. The immaculate track surface had been laid to an incredible accuracy of just a couple of millimetres across its width.

It's not, perhaps, the most obvious place to launch the all-new Subaru Impreza WRX STi. I did wonder whether a road car inspired by a rally car would be best sampled while it was trying to do an impression of a circuit car.

In an ideal world, I suppose, we'd have been given a set of STi keys and enjoyed a late-night strop along the elevated expressways of the megacity that is Tokyo. But this isn't an ideal world, so we have the privilege of eight laps of the circuit that just four weeks before had seen Lewis Hamilton take pole, set a new lap record and eventually win in torrential conditions.

Our day at the track opens reasonably bright and clear, with Mount Fuji visible under the whipping cloud base. A row of STis is lined up in front of the pits. There's no doubt that this car is dramatically different from the stock Impreza.

The STi is 55mm wider than the base version – though it looks much more – and has 45mm and 40mm wider front and rear tracks. Massively extended wings front and rear, a substantial tailgate spoiler and a new bumper design transform the bearing of the car, taking it a long way from the pinched appearance of the original.

The STi sits foursquare and has more than a hint of late-model Lancia Delta Integrale about it, emphasised by the rear wing. But from the evidence lined up in front of us, this heavily reworked look is still less than it could be. The STi's styling seems to me to be particularly sensitive to colour and wheel design.

Dark anthracite grey paint with anthracite 18in five-spoke wheels would seem to be the best of a variable bunch. But it's the car's rear light clusters that continue to offend the eye. Although the chrome boot strip has been lost, the *Max Power* lamps detract greatly from the car's overall appearance.

Inside one of the pit garages an STi is separated into its two main components: the bodyshell and the running gear. If you have a technical bent, this is always a treat, especially when you have the engineers responsible on tap for explanation.

The bodyshell of the STi differs in some significant ways from the stock Impreza, according to the man in charge of it. Because of the substantial extra forces being put on the body via the suspension, extra reinforcement was needed. The main change was inside the rear-hatch aperture.

Unlike previous Imprezas, this new model effectively has a very substantial hole in the structure. Forces from the suspension tend to affect the hatchback aperture, distorting it sideways. The solution was to weld extra stiffening plates onto the inside of the upper corners of the aperture.

'THE FOURSQUARE STi HAS MORE THAN A HINT OF LATE-MODEL LANCIA DELTA INTEGRALE ABOUT IT'

FEATURE

7 NOVEMBER 2007

Volume 254

No 6 | 5766

ABOVE There's a big shove around 4,000rpm.

OPPOSITE Good-looking body, but flawed by ugly light clusters.

BELOW Swish seats, disappointing dash.

Surprisingly, these extra forces (and probably the extra power) also tend to distort the rear chassis rails, leading to them twisting along their length. To prevent this movement (which greatly affects ride and handling because it allows the suspension geometry to be distorted under hard driving) extra plates have been welded to the ends of the rail, where they exit through the rear of the body structure, directly behind the bumper.

At the front, higher forces from the suspension are also dealt with by more reinforcement. A rigid rod is fixed between the base of the A-pillar (behind the front wheel) and the underside of the front chassis rail (which runs above the front wheel). There's also some minor beefing up around the frame that holds the radiator.

However, the new Impreza is actually lighter than the old model, despite a much stronger chassis. Dropping the front subframe has saved around 20–25kg.

Under the skin is Subaru's unique drivetrain, which couples a flat-four boxer engine with 'symmetrical' four-wheel drive, the latter being an arrangement very similar to that used by most Audi Quattros.

Here, the six-speed gearbox is located between the front wheels, with a pair of driveshafts connected to the front wheels and a propshaft running the rear differential, powering the rear wheels. The boxer engine sits ahead of the front axle.

The STi gets a centre viscous coupling and limited-slip differentials front and rear. The rear multi-link suspension is new to this generation of Impreza, as are the aluminium lower suspension arms. The front suspension struts remain inverted.

The engine sits 22mm lower and the centre differential has been lowered by 10mm. Brembo brakes are fitted, with four-pot calipers at the front and twin-pot at the rear, backed up by a more rigid brake system and 'super-low expansion' brake hoses.

The cars on demonstration duty at Fuji are Japanese-spec STis, which means a 2.0-litre flat-four engine fitted with a twin-scroll turbocharger and bigger intercooler. Fitted with AVCS (Active Valve Control System, working on both inlet and exhaust) it's good for 304bhp at 6,400rpm (up 28bhp over the old model) and 311lb ft at 4,400rpm. Subaru says that the engine gives "massive" torque at the bottom end and yet can still be strung out to 8,000rpm.

"Equal length, constant pulsation" exhaust pipes are said to improve torque and throttle response, but also silence the engine's distinctive flat-four thrum. According to the engine graph, the torque delivery takes off in a near-vertical way from 1,500rpm, topping off at around 2,700rpm and climbing

very slightly between there and 4,500rpm, before dropping off steeply.

So with an XL crash helmet squeezed onto my head, I feed myself into the cabin of the Impreza waiting on the Fuji pit lane. Subaru has clearly refused to give in to demands that cars should get ever wider. It's reasonably snug in here.

New seats are welcome, although this car is fitted with the swish optional Recaros. STi logos are scattered across the interior, which is improved over the base car thanks to the use of leather and suede and the upmarket graphite hue in the background. The dash itself is still disappointingly hard-faced and the rest of the switchgear is no more than respectable. Interestingly, the new centre console detail – which holds the ECU and suspension controls – is much more classy. A sign that we might reasonably hope, perhaps, for an eventual facelift.

Pressing the starter button and selecting first, I get an enthusiastic 'go' signal from a Subaru man

'ON THE ENGINE GRAPH, TORQUE DELIVERY TAKES OFF IN A NEAR-VERTICAL WAY FROM 1,500RPM'

HOT AND HOTTER

MAKE	SUBARU IMPREZA	SUBARU IMPREZA
Model	**WRX**	**WRX STi (J SPEC)**
Price	£19,995	£27,000 (est)
0–62mph	6.1sec	4.9sec (est)
Top speed	130mph	158mph
Power	228bhp at 5,200rpm	303bhp at 6,400rpm
Torque	236lb ft at 2,800rpm	311lb ft at 4,400rpm
Power to weight	163bhp per tonne	205bhp per tonne
Torque to weight	169lb ft per tonne	210lb ft per tonne
CO_2 emissions	246g/km	na
Fuel econ (comb)	27.2mpg	na
Length	4,415mm	4,415mm
Width	1,740mm	1,795mm
Height	1,475mm	1,475mm
Wheelbase	2,625mm	2,625mm
Weight	1,395kg	1,480kg
Engine layout	2,457cc, 4 cyls, horizontally opposed, turbocharged petrol	1,994cc, 4 cycls, horizontally opposed, turbocharged petrol
Installation	Front, longitudinal, four-wheel drive	Front, longitudinal, four-wheel drive
Specific output	92.8 bhp per litre	151.9bhp per litre
Compression ratio	8.4:1	13.0:1
Gearbox	5-spd manual	6-spd manual

Body is only slightly wider than regular Impreza, but lower suspension aids purposeful stance.

and hoof off down the pit lane. I stare at the green light just ahead of the exit. This is the F1 view; it feels weird.

I'm no track expert, but I know enough to realise that wide-open expanses – and there are plenty at Fuji – distort the sensation of driving a powerful road car. At the first right-hand bend, it is necessary to slow right down before opening the flat-four's taps and experiencing the STi's 300bhp, which still feels relatively pedestrian.

This engine's delivery is very linear – to the point of feeling a little flat – but you can feel a distinct kick at just over 4,000rpm as the power and torque curves cross. The unit is also very happy to rev right up to the high 7,000s – although a red LED on the rev counter face demands a sharp upshift from the driver.

The brakes feel solid and efficient underfoot, though perhaps a little dead and lacking in feel. The steering, too, doesn't stick in my mind while I struggle with Fuji's mighty sweeping bends and tricky left- and right-handed uphill grades. It is, though, accurate and pointy enough to allow the car to be placed quite readily, right on the red-and-white apex points.

But the most overwhelming memory from my brief eight-lap experience is the Impreza STi's extraordinary ability to hang on, despite the most massive provocation.

Understeer is hardly in evidence, although the car is soft enough to roll quite markedly. It is possible to drive into very long, tight bends and, as long as you stay hard on the gas, the STi will peel around, unwilling to unstick.

Indeed, such are the efforts of other drivers that rubber is peeled off and fired, bung-like, into the wheel housings. I leave with the strong conviction that it would be very hard to lose this car on a road that is well surfaced and dry. It also strikes me that the STi feels immensely rigid.

This Impreza would, though, clearly benefit from the more flexible nature promised by the UK-spec 2.5-litre engine. Although this 2.0-litre unit has the legs, on the road it could lack the sort of in-gear wallop ideal for UK driving.

The WRX STi arrives in the UK next Spring with a price tag upwards of £25k and, unlike the plain WRX, it will not be in limited numbers. The UK car is different enough, and our first encounter unreal enough, for us to reserve final judgement, other than to say that this could turn out to be a very accomplished road car indeed.

THE CRAZE TWIN HOW DOES THE WRX COMPARE?

So where does all this leave the Impreza WRX? Prior to the STi's official touchdown next spring, a limited number of the cheaper and less powerful WRX will be coming in – yours for £19,995. But a first drive over UK roads gives us a chance to see how it compares with the distinctly underwhelming naturally aspirated versions that we've driven so far.

After poring over pics of the STi's chunky contours and tech-laden spec sheet, it's impossible not to feel short-changed by the far less visually arresting propostion of the WRX. Despite the turbocharged performance that lurks beneath, aesthetically the WRX is far closer to the boggo versions than the STi, doing without blistered wheelarches or the full-spec car's aggressive bodykit. Apart from the gaping mono-nostril that sits on top of the bonnet feeding the intercooler (and encouraging jokes about cocaine-ravaged Z-list celebs) it looks pretty much identical to the normally aspirated 2.0 RX version.

The lack of specialness extends into the cabin, where you'll find the same scratchy surfaces, hard-feel plastics, lack of space and old-school stereo display that have already come in for criticism on lesser Imprezas. The difference here is the level of expectation brought with the pricetag: for 20 grand, you would be justified in expecting far better.

Performance is far more persuasive. It's great to find the Subaru flat-four thrum now combined with the familiar surge of a turbocharged mid-range. The WRX's 2.5-litre motor isn't going to break any specific output records – the peak 228bhp emerges from the calculator as just 92.8bhp per litre. But power is delivered with a gutsy enthusiasm familiar from previous turbocharged Subarus. The sense of decontenting stays here, though, given that there are just five gear ratios to choose between rather than the six of the STi.

On the road this Impreza impresses and perplexes in almost equal measure. Over the sort of broken, twisty, greasy B-roads that Scoobies have always shined on, it remains a fine-driving machine. Ride quality is exemplary; generous suspension travel and firm dampers working together to neutralise bumps and dips to an impressive degree. The steering is low-geared but accurate and grip levels are high.

The problem is that roll levels are high, too. The WRX doesn't feel any more stiffly suspended than the 2.0 RX that we put through a full road test, sharing with that car a tendency for surprising levels of roll under hard cornering. Underneath this the WRX hangs on gamefully enough, the slightly rear-biased torque delivery of the four-wheel-drive system helping to tighten the line around longer corners. The brakes are also a big disappointment; cheap single-pot calipers replace the previous WRX four-pot front stoppers. Even on moderately hard road driving, fade arrives early. It just doesn't feel anything like as dynamically focused as a Mégane R26 or a Focus ST.

And that's the WRX's biggest problem. By turning this generation of Impreza into a hatchback, Subaru is encouraging direct comparison between the WRX and the latest crop of hot hatches. And with dowdy styling and no more performance than the quickest of its front-driven rivals, this Impreza feels too expensive and not quite special enough.

PACE CADETS

The new Subaru Impreza WRX has been transformed in every way. But can it now live with the best hot hatches? Richard Bremner decides

WRX. GTI. Both confections of letters trigger immediate dreams of hard driving adventure in the heads of car nuts across the planet. But quite which part of the Renault Mégane Renaultsport 230 F1 Team R26's gloriously excessive name we're meant to latch onto is hard to know. But latch we will, because this car is our current king of the hill in the hot hatch world. It's certainly strong enough to topple the Golf, if a ferocious drive along a British back road is your criterion. The VW fights back in other ways, as we shall see, but it now has another hatch to see off, or not, in the shape of Subaru's latest Impreza WRX.

What we have here, then, are the lairy, the civilised and the odd. The lairy is the Renault, of course, and not just because of its vibrant yellow paint, its unusually large alloys, its twin exhausts, some very odd stickers and a pair of no-messing race seats which trumpet its road-weapon message as effectively as a politician's battle-bus megaphone.

Were it not whiter than a celebrity's teeth, this Golf would be distinguishable as a GTi only by those in the know, even if it sports fashionable red brake calipers and a different grille. This is a car for going fast less obviously, although it can achieve point-to-point speeds just as well as the Renault and Subaru.

It's the Impreza, of course, which is odd. Odd to look at, its dated silhouette further undermined by crude sill extensions emphasising a too-narrow track, strange rear lights and a troubled face, and odd mechanically with its boxer engine and all-wheel-drive traction.

But in terms of straight road ability the WRX kicks off with an immediate advantage. It has the same 227bhp power output as the Renault, both of these eclipsing the Golf's 197bhp (you can have a 227bhp Golf GTi Edition 30, but you'll need £22,322). All

three achieve these lofty figures with turbochargers, although the Impreza also relies on extra capacity. Not that this gives it much of a torque advantage over the muscular Renault. It also loses out with a five-speed transmission to the six-speeders sported by the others.

While we're trading mechanical points, both the Subaru and VW benefit from multi-link rear suspension while the Mégane makes do with a simpler twist beam axle. The front-drive cars provide limited-slip differentials, which go some way to countering the firepower of Subaru's permanent all-wheel drive, now with a tighter mechanical limited-slip differential rather than the previous viscous item. It's set up to distribute torque equally to each axle, although it varies depending on the available traction. It's surprising, though, that more torque isn't sent to the rear axle. As you'd expect, all three supplement this hardware with electronic stability control, switchable in every case, to provide a final layer of dynamic protection.

The cabins range from the workmanlike to the subtly inviting. Despite being the newest car here, the Subaru's interior is at best unprepossessing. A gloomy mix of blacks and greys, it is only mildly relieved by the extensive use of faux aluminium ladled on with depressingly little flair. The dashboard is hard-feel, and although logically laid out you'd hardly call it elegant. Sporting kit includes a leather-bound wheel that's actually good to grasp (and equipped with stereo and cruise controls), grippy tombstone bucket seats that look like refugees from a 1970s Japanese coupé and instrument needles that perform an alluring dance before the flat four fires up. The WRX does without the aluminium pedals sported by the others, has cruder seat adjusters and feels built down to a price well below £20k. But aside from a handbrake that worries your left thigh, it's easy to get comfortable.

'PLAY INSIDE THE SLITHERING UNDERSTEER ZONE AND YOU CAN EASILY ADJUST THE WRX'S LINE WITH THE THROTTLE'

FEATURE

28 NOVEMBER 2007

Volume 254

No 9 | 5769

Comfort, and the aura of it, is far more evident in the Golf. Its seats are less extremely styled, though equally supportive, its cabin is fashioned to far higher standards and the inevitable aluminium décor is real and artfully applied. The upper dash is soft-feel, the wheel appeals with its trendy flat bottom and the ambience is one you'll enjoy, even if you wouldn't call it luxurious. It's certainly comfortable, easy to get the seat and wheel arranged just so, and it doesn't make you feel that you've stepped into a car modified for circuit work.

Unlike the Mégane, whose cabin is a curious mix of design flair (what with its striking aluminium door pulls and hooded instrument pack) and track-day special. Its Recaro seats and their black steel pedestals make this car look 'home modified', an impression heightened by its aluminium pedal covers. Those seats feel quite enclosing at first but they turn out to be comfortable on a long run, as are the Subaru's oddly textured chairs.

The Impreza's curious and often endearing character floods in as soon as you turn the key, the flat four's starter making that familiar whooping, high-pitched whirr before it settles to a thrumming idle. Less familiar is the gearchange, the lever now moving with something approaching oiled precision. As soon as you move off, this car feels lively and up for it. A light, goading whine overlays the four's background beat, and the Impreza feels light on its feet and surprisingly deft over small urban bumps. This feels like a car you can get to work with.

So do the Golf and the Renault, except that their potency and athleticism are more masked. Much of the time the R26 possesses a civility entirely at odds with its bucket seats, the engine humming innocuously, its gearlever threading home with little resistance, the chassis absorbing small bumps with unexpected pliancy. The VW feels similar, except its optional 18in alloys add jiggle to a ride that is calmer on the stock 17s. Its gearlever moves with a more mechanical motion and its engine's sporting edge is slightly more evident on a light throttle. Apart from the ride, it feels as civilised as its cabin implies. But crush the throttle in second and you're in for that GTi surprise, this innocuous urban shopper transforming to urgent road eater. In fact, the Golf is the slowest of our trio (no surprise given its horsepower shortfall), but it will break 62mph in 7.2sec, making it brisk enough for a B-road.

But the Subaru's superior traction ensures that it outsprints both cars to 62mph, its spectacular 5.4sec

ABOVE Latest WRX retains plenty of steering feel but needs to send more power to the back wheels.

RIGHT Renault high points are excellent ESP and its composure during B-road blasts.

RIGHT The VW impresses but doesn't inform the driver quite as well as the others.

easily bettering the Renault's 6.2sec. Traction and gearing help the WRX's case, to 62mph at least, because it has only five ratios to the others' six, and they're lower geared too, making it a slightly fussier cruiser at high speeds. On the road the differences are less apparent, all three engines impressive for the speed at which their turbos stir solid low-rev torque. Both Renault and VW engines rev to 7,000rpm, but the R26's charge to the limiter slows over the last 1,000rpm. Both sound smooth doing it, are quiet and issue a reasonably sporting beat. The WRX's engine is busier, that whine almost overwhelming the flat four's warblings, before sounding slightly stressed as it bears down on the 6,800rpm limit. This powertrain is slightly less civilised than the other two but it sounds more interesting.

It's the same mix of qualities that characterise the Subaru's handling. Of course it has great traction, but beware extra-enthusiastic departures from side roads; yours truly had himself a monumental first-gear tail slither that required a lot of road space and arm flailing to collect. An oversteer moment like this might tempt you into thinking that this is an option for trimming the car's trajectory at speed, but short of throwing it into bends like a rally driver,

what you ultimately get is understeer – and lots of it if you're navigating a tight bend or a roundabout in the rain. Which is why it's a shame that the WRX doesn't apportion more torque to the rear wheels. The Subaru is at a disadvantage when you compare its rubber with the other two (the Renault plays 235s to its 205s, for instance) but its ultimate grip is a little disappointing, on wet roads at least.

That doesn't mean it isn't fun. Play inside the slithering understeer zone and you can easily adjust its line on the throttle and enjoy deft, feelsome steering to go with it, as well as a subtly loping ride that deals confidently with big crests and dips. This is where you feel its WRC breeding. It's noisier than the other two, which makes you feel that you're working at it more, and avoiding a terminal understeer moment will keep you sharp (in contrast to the Impreza's ESP, which appears to have the skid perception skills of a dead dog). But it's engaging, and with its loping gait and distinctive soundtrack it feels appealingly different.

Most of the time, though, the Renault makes a better job of blasting over B-roads. The moments when it doesn't are when the road turns particularly rough, its firm suspension unable to deal with staccato bumps without making you feel them too. And if you

ABOVE VW's had plenty of time to get the GTi's cabin right – it's the best of the three; Design flair meets track-day special in the R26 – comfortable too; put simply, WRX's interior doesn't feel like it belongs in a £20k car.

turn off the ESP (there's little point) on a wet road you'll confirm that 230bhp is a lot of grunt to put through the front wheels, the wheel torque-steering slightly over an uneven surface, like the Golf's. But this car is amazingly civilised for one so powerful, powering from bend to bend with an almost languid demeanour that's reinforced only by the lazy ease with which you palm its gearlever about. All of which partially masks an amazing ability on roads like these. As does a deft ESP system that will catch a mild lift-off oversteer moment if you're too slow yourself. Its steering delivers excellent feel, especially for one so wide-tyred; it's quick, precise, and follows cambers to just the right degree.

The Golf, by contrast, delivers tactile sensations that seem to be sheathed in rubber. Yes, it is precise, accurate and confidence-building, and its ESP system is just as effective, but its communication skills aren't as crisp as the Renault's and Subaru's. But again that doesn't mean it isn't entertaining. Like the Renault, it musters more front-end grip than the WRX, scurries about with terrific agility and provides great entertainment. As an all-rounder – and that, surely, is what your versatile hot hatch is supposed to be – it is the most complete car here.

The WRX, although less extreme than its predecessor, is nevertheless a more interesting device to conduct if you can ignore its shortfalls in the furnishing department. It makes more interesting noises, you can do more to alter its line with your right foot and its abilities over roads that demand long suspension travel are truly impressive. Yet it's undermined by a lack of grip and understeer habits that simply aren't present in the other pair, four-wheel drive or not.

The Renault, then, remains supreme, maintaining its lead with its massive, reliable grip, its sensitive steering and unwavering agility, qualities which it blends against an impressive backdrop of refinement, except when the road turns rough. If that puts you off, along with lairy detailing and the aftermarket seats, then the Golf is probably for you. And the Subaru? It continues to be a not-quite-realised talent, undermined in the WRX's case by the final components required to build its grip and kill the understeer, and Subaru's perverse insistence on building cars that are hard on the eye. Still, there's entertainment in pondering which of the interior and exterior are least pleasing to look at, a diversion drivers of the Renault and Golf are denied.

ABOVE New Impreza won't win any beauty contests; Golf is subtle and the R26 wacky.

LAIRY, ODD AND LAID BACK

MAKE	RENAULT MEGANE	SUBARU	VOLKSWAGEN
Model	**RENAULTSPORT 230 F1 TEAM R26**	**IMPREZA WRX**	**GOLF 2.0 T-FSI GTI 3DR**
Price	£19,860	£19,995	£20,607
0–62mph	6.2sec	5.4sec	7.2sec
Top speed	147mph	130mph	146mph
Power	227bhp at 5,500rpm	227bhp at 5,200rpm	197bhp at 5,100rpm
Torque	229lb ft at 3,000rpm	236lb ft at 2,800rpm	207lb ft at 1,800–5,000rpm
Power to weight	169bhp per tonne	163bhp per tonne	148bhp per tonne
Torque to weight	170lb ft per tonne	169lb ft per tonne	156lb ft per tonne
Emissions (CO_2)	200g/km	246g/km	189g/km
Urban	24.4mpg	19.8mpg	25.7mpg
Extra-urban	42.2mpg	34.4mpg	45.6mpg
Combined	33.2mpg	27.2mpg	35.3mpg
Range	438 miles	359 miles	427 miles
Length	4228mm	4,415mm	4,216mm
Width	1,777mm	1,740mm	1,759mm
Height	1,437mm	1,475mm	1,469mm
Wheelbase	2,617mm	2,620mm	2,578mm
Weight	1,345kg	1,395kg	1,328kg
Fuel tank	60 litres	60 litres	55 litres
Boot	330 litres	538 litres	350 litres
Engine layout	4 cyls in line, 1,998cc, turbocharged	4 cyls horizontally opposed, 2,457cc, turbocharged	4 cyls in line, 1,984cc, turbocharged
Installation	Front, transverse, front-wheel drive	Front, longitudinal, all-wheel drive	Front, transverse, front-wheel drive
Specific output	114bhp per litre	92bhp per litre	99bhp per litre
Compression ratio	9.0:1	8.4:1	10.5:1
Gearbox	6-speed manual	5-speed manual	6-speed manual
Front suspension	MacPherson struts, coil springs, anti-roll bar	MacPherson struts, coil springs, anti-roll bar	MacPherson struts, coil springs, anti-roll bar
Rear suspension	Twist beam axle, coil springs, anti-roll bar	Multi-link, coil springs, anti-roll bar	Multi-link, coil springs, anti-roll bar
Brakes	312mm ventilated discs (f) 300mm ventilated discs (r)	Ventilated discs (f) solid discs (r)	Ventilated discs (f) solid discs (r)
Wheels	8.0Jx18in	7.0Jx17in	7.5Jx17in
Tyres	235/40 R18	205/50 R17	225/45 R17

BELOW Much fun can still be had in the Scooby, but that diminishes on wet asphalt.

MENTAL INSTITUTIONS

The Subaru Impreza STi and Mitsubishi Evo are legends, but which of the latest loony twins makes the most sense? Here's an early answer from Japan

The year has barely begun and we're already into one of 2008's most eagerly anticipated comparison tests. This is the first time that the all-new Mitsubishi Lancer Evo X has come up against the car that's set to become its arch enemy: Subaru's Impreza STi.

Of course, this story will only conclude when we get these two cars in UK spec and sharing the same bit of British road. But for the early steer on the hottest super-saloon battle we've opted to bring two Japanese-spec versions together on some of Japan's most challenging driving roads. Which is why the tale starts heading west out of Tokyo, dodging the trucks, Crowns and Cedrics that fill the crowded freeway.

There's history here. Hot Lancers and Imprezas have played tag throughout the past decade; time and again there have been newer and madder versions to tempt and tease us, yet neither has ever managed to quite escape the other. Each has been brilliant in its own right, but now the game has moved on. And with an increased emphasis on comfort and usability, the biggest question has to be whether both have kept their souls.

Let's start with the Evo, appearing here in Japan's top domestic GSR spec. This is the first truly new Evo since the original appeared in 1992, without a carry-over part in sight. Now there's a fresh platform, bodyshell, engine, transmission, chassis and four-wheel-drive system. All of this was developed at a time when the company was racking up massive losses and its very survival was hanging by a pretty slender thread. The Evo is crucial to Mitsubishi's image and reputation.

The end result rises far beyond its humble Lancer origins, the muscular design building well on the cooking saloon that lurks beneath. It's more elegant than its brutish predecessors, a little Italian in places but with an inverted slant nose and a trapezoidal grille that still lend the right air of visual aggression, as do the flared wheel arches and mandatory boot spoiler. You could imagine this Evo tempting wavering Alfa or even BMW buyers into the fold.

TWIN TEST

16 JANUARY 2008

Volume 255

No 3 | 5775

Yet Subaru has arguably gambled much more with its decision to switch the Impreza from a saloon to a hatchback body. At the level of cooking versions, it's fair to say the jury is still unconvinced. But the STi was overseen by a different designer, one given free rein to make substantial changes. Most of the body panels are new, with pumped-out arches, a new grille, twin pipes, a chunky bonnet hump and – of course – another spoiler that clings to the top of the tailgate. It looks great in the metal, especially wearing these finned, gold 18-inch BBS alloys and finished in the classic WRC blue.

Under the surface it is far closer to being an evolved version of the previous Impreza – no bad thing in itself. That means forest stage-friendly struts at each corner, a turbocharged flat four motor mounted low down at the front of the car and a developed version of Subaru's all-wheel-drive system. The shell has been stiffened, the suspension has been upgraded and the fat alloys and wide tracks prove that it means business.

KEEPING THE FUN FACTOR

The first driving impressions are harvested before we've even left the freeway; both cars have really grown up. Much of the dynamic aggression has been dialled out and a new level of refinement has found its way in.

BELOW STi is definitely the best-looking of the new breed of Impreza; WRC blue Scooby with gold BBS rims? Some traditions live on.

The good news is that this added sophistication hasn't come at the expense of the raw amusement to be wrought from flinging either car down a twisty road. Both still have the ability to dispatch corners and compressions with the sort of ease and speed

ABOVE There is a subtlety to some of the Evo's performance ad-ons.

LEFT New Evo is a big car but it's more elegant than previous models.

ABOVE New-school Evo feels decidedly old-school inside; it's pretty poor.

RIGHT Interior is the Evo's weakest point by far; at least its length results in decent rear legroom and a proper boot.

that would leave supercars floundering. Perhaps there isn't that raw involvement there once was, but across country we'd wager the new cars will be quicker because they can hang on for longer, shrug off more extreme manoeuvres, and in the STi's case because it bangs out more power. What's not to like?

The Mitsubishi's all-new aluminium 2.0-litre four keeps variable valve timing and is claimed to be lighter, torquier, cleaner and more frugal than the previous Evo's powerplant. Power is still capped at a conservative 276bhp in Japan, but UK-spec versions will have 295bhp and the prospect of more to come with the inevitable FQ versions.

Even in its lowest-power form the motor sports a wide powerband, boosting smoothly and progressively from 1,500rpm onwards. It lacks the characterful brutality of the old engine – and also its predecessor's ultra-sharp throttle response – but it's strong, punchy and businesslike.

Our Evo came with the optional High Performance Package, bringing Bilstein dampers, Evo IX MR-style Eibach sports springs, lightweight Brembo brakes and ultra-grippy 18-inch Yokohama tyres. But the biggest part of its dynamic arsenal comes through the introduction of 'Super All-Wheel Control' (S-AWC) and Active Stability Control, over and above the Active Centre Diff, Sports ABS and Active Yaw Control rear diff that previous Evos offered. The idea behind all of these integrated systems is to optimise the distribution of drive torque and brake force at each wheel. As before, the driver's main input into proceedings comes with the three-mode switch that allows a choice between tarmac, gravel and snow modes.

S-AWC sounds complicated, and it is. But the systems know when to fade into the background and let you get on with the business of driving, giving fabulously agile handling and a chassis exploitable enough to make anyone feel like a hero.

The Mitsubishi's turn-in is razor sharp, grip is massive and the natural balance is impressively neutral. Even when the car is thrown into a slippery, tightening bend, the systems do an outstanding job of keeping you on a chosen line, over bumps that would have thrown a previous-gen Evo wide. It feels better tied down than the previous car, grippier at both ends and much easier to control at extremes. At the limit understeer arrives eventually, but with ASC switched on the Evo feels impossible to spin. Drift merchants might prefer the old car, but the new Evo is still a hugely satisfying drive.

Our test Evo X came with the old-school five-speed manual transmission, which feels very old-fashioned in comparison with the rest of the car with its wide gate and sloppy shift movement. Previous experience with the six-speed SST twin-clutch unit suggests that it's a far better prospect, with near-instantaneous shifts delivered at the command of the magnesium paddle shifters, and three different modes.

FIGURES WITH FEELING

Step from the Evo and into the STi and you enter a different world. The Mitsubishi's interior still feels very old-fashioned next to modern European rivals, both in terms of a slightly dated design but also the shockingly low-rent materials from which it is made. Subaru's mission to elevate the Impreza's quality to a level competitive with cars like the Golf might not have been entirely successful, but it feels a league ahead here. Both Evo and STi boast optional front Recaro buckets, which work well in both cars and combine excellent support with decent driving positions. But it's the STi's Alcantara-and-leather-trimmed cabin that feels like a far classier proposition than the Mitsubishi's.

The Japanese STi gets a hard-charging 2.0-litre flat four motor with a twin-scroll turbo, now good for 304bhp. European versions will stick with a bigger-capacity 2.5-litre unit with a single-scroll turbo and, at 297bhp, slightly less power.

To be honest, there's little reason to be disappointed. The smaller-capacity boxer revs harder and higher, with a definite bump in the performance curve around 4,000rpm to add some character. But the 2.5, now with variable valve timing on both the inlet and exhaust, is more linear, more characterful and benefits from better transmission of Subaru's trademark throbbing exhaust note. While it revs to 'only' 6,700rpm, compared with the 2.0-litre unit's 8,000rpm redline, there's plenty of torque at low revs and power is delivered more smoothly.

That's by the by for now, of course; our Japanese car has to fight the Evo with its 2.0-litre unit. At least the transmission is common between Japan and the UK, with the same six-speed manual unit from the outgoing model being carried over. It's got a quality, workmanlike feel to the shift action, but as before it can get tight and notchy if you try to rush it. And there are no plans for a twin-clutch or auto 'box.

On paper, the STi's chassis has it all. Not only has it been widened and fitted with sticky 18-inch Bridgestone Potenzas, but the driver-controlled centre differential (DCCD) has also been improved and now acts more quickly to transfer different amounts of

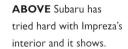

ABOVE Subaru has tried hard with Impreza's interior and it shows.

LEFT Hatchback practicality for the latest STi; the interior's still not up to regular VW Golf standards, though.

TECHNO SPECS

MAKE	MITSUBISHI	SUBARU
Model	**LANCER EVOLUTION X GSR**	**IMPREZA WRX STi**
Price in UK	£27,499	£24,995
Price in Japan	¥3.495 million (£15,304)	¥3.654 million (£16,004)
On sale in UK	February 2008	March 2008
0–62mph	5.0sec (est)	4.9sec (est)
Top speed	150mph (est)	150mph (est)
Power	276bhp at 6,500rpm	304bhp at 6,400rpm
Torque	311lb ft at 3,500rpm	311lb ft at 4,400rpm
Emissions (CO_2)	na	na
Economy (Japanese '10.15-mode' cycle)	27.9mpg	29.4mpg
Range	338 miles	388 miles
Length	4,495mm	4,415mm
Width	1,810mm	1,795mm
Height	1,480mm	1,475mm
Wheelbase	2,650mm	2,625mm
Kerb weight	1,470kg	1,480kg
Fuel tank	55 litres	60 litres
Boot (max)	323 litres	538 litres
Engine layout	4 cyls in line, 1,998cc, turbocharged	4 cyls horizontally opposed, 1,994cc (Japan spec), twin-scroll turbocharged
Installation	Longitudinal, front, four-wheel drive	Longitudinal, front, four-wheel drive
Specific output	138bhp per litre	152bhp per litre
Compression ratio	9.0:1	8.0:1
Gearbox	5-speed manual	6-speed manual
Front suspension	MacPherson struts, coil springs, anti-roll bar	MacPherson struts, coil springs, anti-roll bar
Rear suspension	Multi-link, coil springs, anti-roll bar	Double wishbones, coil springs, anti-roll bar
Brakes	Brembo, ventilated discs (f/r)	Brembo, ventilated discs (f/r)
Wheels	8.5J x 18in, alloy	8.5J x 18in, alloy
Tyres	245/40 R18	245/40 R18

torque between the front and rear axles. Complicating matters further is the arrival of Subaru's new VSA stability control system, which can be left on, turned entirely off or partially engaged to change the point at which it decides to intervene.

Irrespective of how you play around with these settings, the STi feels quite different from the Evo. For a start, there's a stiffness to the Scooby's chassis that takes some getting used to after spending time in the more compliant Mitsubishi. You'll also find that you feel slightly more detached from the driving process, thanks to the weightier steering and less exploitable chassis balance. Its limits are massively high, and the STi hangs on like pretty much nothing else. But over Japanese mountain roads, it lacks the magic connection that the Evo manages to make with its driver.

BEYOND THE RAW TECH

The über-Impreza is certainly a far more sophisticated driving device than the hardcore STis of old; the ride quality is better too. It could be that you need a track day and a wide, open corner to get the very best out of the variable DCCD settings. But it's also true that

on dry roads at vaguely sane speeds, the differences between front and rear-biased torque settings are not particularly noticeable.

The real difference comes when you turn the VSA off. Then the STi becomes less impressive than the Mitsubishi: less precise, less accurate and with less bite. This isn't meant to denigrate the Impreza, though; it's still an amazingly effective way of covering ground at a serious pace. The strong, fade-free brakes are worthy of particular praise.

But with all the provisos about Japanese spec and Japanese roads read into the record, here's the deal: the Subaru just isn't as much fun as the Evo. Both cars are packed with astonishing amounts of technology, but it's the Mitsubishi that manages to feel simpler, more instant and more down-to-earth when being driven in the manner in which these cars are made to be driven.

On a twisty road it's an absolute five-star joy, and British petrolheads should be slobbering with anticipation of its arrival. Yes, the STi is better made, more refined and less boy racer-ish. We suspect it is ultimately faster too. But it's first blood to the Evo. Prepare to want one.

ABOVE Both cars have been developed with an increased emphasis on comfort and usability.

OPPOSITE Evo's four-pot (top) is good for 295bhp in UK spec; STi's 2.0-litre boxer is for Japan only.

SUBARU IMPREZA STi

Does the STi turn the latest, less extreme, incarnation of the Impreza into a proper driver's tool? We put Subaru's latest offering through its paces

The arrival of this latest-generation Impreza has been an event tinged with contrary feelings of faint regret and hopeful anticipation. Regret that this new-generation five-door version of the legendary boxer-engined B-road blaster is barely any better looking than the last, if at all, and anticipation that as Subaru rolls out progressively more powerful versions, the resulting confection will be a little more appealing.

This WRX STi certainly gets off to a better start by providing more power, more toys, a new multi-link rear axle, an upgraded four-wheel-drive system and a better furnished interior, all for £1,600 less than the outgoing car cost. And it also looks better than the lesser five-doors, its case helped by its blistered wheel arches, fatter wheels, an air intake big enough to ingest a modest swarm of locusts and a prominent tail spoiler.

The issue, then, is whether this latest hot Impreza has the hardware to outpoint the latest Mitsubishi Evo – and whether the sanitisation of its manners can tempt buyers from less extreme machinery.

DESIGN AND ENGINEERING ★★★★

This new Impreza body might be a five-door hatch to the previous iteration's choice of four-door saloon or estate, but the mechanical make-up of the Impreza

QUICK FACTS

Model	Impreza 2.5 WRX STi
Price	£24,995
Power	296bhp
Torque	300lb ft
0–60mph	5.2sec
Fuel economy	18.1mpg
CO_2 emissions	243g/km
70–0mph	50.6m
Skidpan	0.81g

ROAD TEST

5 MARCH 2008

Volume 255

No 10 | 5782

ABOVE Back bumper has been reshaped for STi to reduce lift. No giant-size single exhaust here; you get four pipes, their plumbing claimed to reduce back pressure by 38 per cent.

OPPOSITE STi's 17in alloys are slightly overwhelmed by the blistered wheel arches, so this Impreza still looks under-wheeled; flat four engine lowers centre of gravity for more agile handling; the STi engine now sits 22mm lower at the nose, while the differential is 10mm lower.

HISTORY

The Impreza family tree sprouted in 1992, and a complicated thing it is too, with endless iterations whose codenames (P1, 22B, RB5, RB320, WRX, STi, V-Limited) are the stuff of enthusiasts' nods, winks and knowing grins. The second-generation version arrived in 2000, distinguished by an unfortunate bug-eyed look exorcised by a Peter Stevens facelift in 2003, then another in 2005 that also brought the 2.5-litre engine.

Bug-eyed look was universally disliked; didn't last long

has remained throughout: a flat four engine (often turbocharged) driving all four wheels to win Subaru many a World Rally Championship and a reputation for hardcore, affordable performance cars rivalled only by Mitsubishi.

The flat four keeps the car's centre of gravity low and sharpens its agility, while the drivetrain's longitudinal layout makes it easier to provide full-time four-wheel drive. But this time around the body is more space-efficient. It's shorter but rides on a longer wheelbase (by 93mm) and wider tracks to provide more room inside, while the new multi-link rear suspension (essentially double wishbones with additional control links) packages more compactly to provide a bigger boot. The new car weighs a little more than the old one, though, coming in at 1,530kg on MIRA's scales versus 1,493kg for the old car, and 58 per cent of that lies over the front wheels.

The 2.5-litre boxer engine is essentially the same as before, but a larger intercooler and variable valve timing lift its output by 20bhp to 296bhp, and the torque curve fattens slightly to peak 11lb ft higher at 300lb ft. It's hooked up to a six-speed gearbox and an all-wheel-drive set-up that apportions torque front to rear via a viscous coupling, and from side

to side using mechanical limited-slip differentials, as with the previous STi. Also carried over, with mild modifications, is Subaru's Driver Control Centre Differential (DCCD) which enables you to alter the amount of torque apportioned to the axles, to enhance either straight-line stability or the car's agility through corners. And this is overlaid with adjustable throttle mapping, called Si-Mode.

INTERIOR ★★☆

The good news is that this interior is better than the last Impreza's. The bad news is that it isn't good enough for the class and certainly not for a car costing £25k. If Subaru is serious about widening this car's appeal to drivers less willing to sacrifice everything for the driving experience, it will have to try harder; plenty of superminis costing half the money have cabins that are more appealingly styled, fabricated and finished than this.

But it's an improvement, and if the sculpture of the main dashboard moulding looks a little odd, it has more substance about it than that of the previous car. The leather and Alcantara sports seats look more appealing than those of lesser Imprezas,

ROAD TEST SUBARU IMPREZA WRX STi

ACCELERATION Dry track, 14°C

30mph	40	50	60	70	80	90	100	110	120	130
1.6s	2.7s	3.7s	5.2s	6.6s	8.6s	10.6s	12.9s	16.6s	20.6s	25.8s

DRY/WET BRAKING 60–0mph 3.03sec

30mph-0	30mph-0	50mph-0	50mph-0	Dry 70mph-0	Wet 70mph-0
8.9m	9.3m	25.0m	25.8m	50.6m	63.7m

ACCELERATION IN GEAR

MPH	2nd	3rd	4th	5th	6th
20–40	2.1	3.6	6.4	12.3	15.2
30–50	1.8	2.7	4.8	7.7	12.3
40–60	-	2.5	3.7	6.1	10.6
50–70	-	2.6	3.5	5.1	8.9
60–80	-	-	3.7	4.9	7.7
70–90	-	-	4.0	5.4	7.5
80–100	-	-	4.5	6.1	7.8
90–110	-	-	-	7.1	8.6
100–120	-	-	-	8.1	-
110–130	-	-	-	9.6	-
120–140	-	-	-	-	-

MAX SPEED IN GEAR

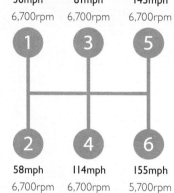

36mph	81mph	145mph
6,700rpm	6,700rpm	6,700rpm
①	③	⑤
②	④	⑥
58mph	114mph	155mph
6,700rpm	6,700rpm	5,700rpm

ECONOMY

	TEST		CLAIMED	
Average	18.1mpg	Urban	20.5mpg
Touring	23.5mpg	Ex-urb	34.4mpg
Track	6.3mpg	Comb	27.4mpg
Tank size	60 litres	Test range	240 miles

CABIN NOISE

Idle 48dB **Max revs in 3rd** 76dB **30mph** 67dB
50mph 70dB **70mph** 72dB

SAFETY

ABS, EBD, VDC

EuroNCAP crash rating	na
Pedestrian rating	na

GREEN RATING

CO_2 emissions	243g/km
Tax at 22/40% pcm	£160/£291

TESTER'S NOTES

RICHARD BREMNER The tailgate needed a hefty slam, on the test car at least, to engage the second catch that stops it rattling.

JAMIE CORSTORPHINE Subarus have been distinguished by frameless door glass for decades, but this Impreza has frames for the first time.

MATT PRIOR The STi is the first car since we shifted our testing to MIRA that has required refuelling mid-test.

JOBS FOR THE FACELIFT

- Sports front seats could do with lumbar adjusters. It's quite an omission in a car of this price, and one you'll feel after an hour or two.
- Upgrade the interior quality, again. It's better, but well adrift of the class best – from the class below.

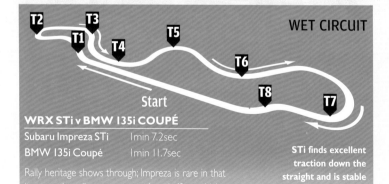

DRY CIRCUIT

Start
T7 T1 T6 T2 T4 T5 T3

WRX STi v BMW 135i COUPÉ

Subaru Impreza STi	1min 18.4sec
BMW 135i Coupé	1min 20.9sec

Driven at 80 per cent, the Impreza is a curiously unsatisfying, understeer-biased device; it takes real commitment to unlock all of its potential.

The STi is fast but its brakes withstand stern use well, although they will eventually fade on track.

WET CIRCUIT

T2 T3 T1 T4 T5 T6 T8 T7
Start

WRX STi v BMW 135i COUPÉ

Subaru Impreza STi	1min 7.2sec
BMW 135i Coupé	1min 11.7sec

Rally heritage shows through; Impreza is rare in that it responds well to even more throttle if you think you've overcooked a corner, finding amazing traction.

STi finds excellent traction down the straight and is stable under high-speed braking into first corner.

the steering wheel is a pleasing thing to grasp and the pre-start dance performed by the instrument needles (which can be programmed out) is a pleasing visual diversion. There's also plenty of room up front (notwithstanding a handbrake that can dig at bigger legs), fair room in the back, a large and well shaped boot and plenty of cubbies and cup-holders. The stereo sounds good too, the climate control is simple but effective and all the major controls are easily manipulated. But despite being practical and well provisioned, the interior of an Impreza remains a disappointing place – especially when Subaru has shown it can do better with the Legacy.

PERFORMANCE ★★★★

It doesn't feel like you have 296bhp under your right toe the first time you drive this car, which feels fast but not wildly so. But you'll eventually realise that the Subaru's 'sport' throttle mode – adjusted via a large rotary knob on the centre console – is actually the equivalent of 'normal'. So the flat four's responses are more languid and this, coupled with the need to wind the turbo up, makes the STi feel slightly lazy. But thoughts of slothfulness are instantly banished

when you turn the knob to 'sport sharp' and mash the throttle, the flat four producing the kind of urgent zest you'd expect. The aural accompaniment improves too, an eager, sawing overlay of sound mixing with the boxer's familiar whirr, whine and warble, although at higher revs it sounds less distinctive than before, the famous Subaru beat almost extinguished.

Beyond 4,000rpm the engine is pulling with such

ABOVE STi looks a lot beefier than the WRX, but 18in wheels would be better.

BELOW Boot is relatively shallow but can be extended by splitting/ folding rear seats.

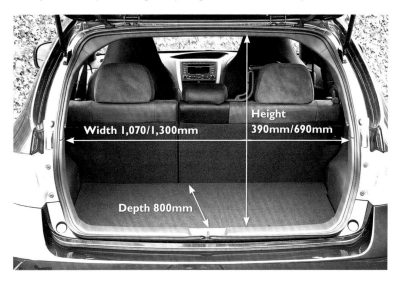

Width 1,070/1,300mm
Height 390mm/690mm
Depth 800mm

Rotary climate controls deliver excellent temperature stratification, although ultimate output could be greater and there's no side-to-side split.

You get a temperature gauge, in contrast to the lesser RX, but no oil temperature gauge. Rev counter is small, but there's a change-up light.

INSTANT GROUP TEST

MAKE	RENAULTSPORT	MITSUBISHI	BMW	SUBARU
Model	**Mégane R26**	**Evo X GS FQ-300**	**135i M Sport Coupé**	**Impreza WRX STi**
Price	£19,895	£27,499	£29,745	£24,995
Power	227bhp at 5,500rpm	291bhp at 6,500rpm	302bhp at 5,800rpm	296bhp at 6,000rpm
Torque	229lb ft at 3,000rpm	300lb ft at 3,850rpm	295lb ft at 1,300–5,000rpm	300lb ft at 4,000rpm
0–60mph	6.2sec (claimed to 62mph)	4.7sec (claimed to 62mph)	5.4sec	5.2sec
Top speed	147mph (claimed)	150mph (claimed)	155mph (claimed)	155mph (claimed)
Fuel consumption	33.2mpg (combined)	27.4mpg (combined)	30.7mpg (combined)	27.4mpg (combined)
Kerb weight	1,355kg	1,560kg	1,560kg	1,530kg
CO_2/tax band	200g/km, 27 per cent	246g/km, 35 per cent	220g/km, 31 per cent	243g/km, 35 per cent
We think	A proper driver's car; differential transforms it through the bends..	As devastatingly fast as ever, and now much easier to live with.	Pricey and not quite as focused as we'd hoped, but what an engine.	More rounded than the old STi, but not as good as it could have been.
VERDICT	★★★★	★★★★	★★★★	★★★☆

urgency that you'll need a hand on the gearlever in readiness for the rev limit's 6,700rpm arrival and the glowering change-up light that precedes it. If you're too slow, you'll hit a slightly savage limiter. Rapid clutch action gets you clean shifts and you'll be romping towards the danger paint again and the easy 100mph gait that the Impreza feels comfortable with, even if you and your licence won't.

The figures bear out these sensations, even if our numbers didn't match the 4.8sec 0–60mph claim, our car needing 5.2sec in near-dry conditions. We imagine that in the wet it would be able to spin all four wheels from rest and get rather closer to the claimed time. But this is still damned fast – almost a second swifter than the Renault Mégane R26's 6.1sec and the Golf R32's 6.0sec. That said, the Mitsubishi Evo GSR and the BMW 135i coupé are in the hunt at around 5.0sec dead. The Impreza's in-gear times ram home the fact that you need revs and a spinning blower to get the best from it; 30–50mph in fourth requires 4.8sec, but 40–60mph, 50–70mph and 60–80mph are each dispatched in under four seconds.

There's a third setting for that throttle map control; pressing the knob gets an 'intelligent' strategy that adjusts the engine's responsiveness to suit your driving style, but we could detect little advantage. Subaru would be better directed

to eliminate the driveline shunt caused by the slow-slow-sudden decay of revs when you lift off and coast, and unprogressive tip-in when the accelerator is reapplied.

WHAT IT COSTS

SUBARU IMPREZA WRX STi

On-the-road price	£24,995	
Price as tested	£25,490	
Value after 3yrs	na	
Typical PCP pcm	na	
Contract hire pcm	na	
Cost per mile	na	
Insurance/typical quote	19/£796	

MP3/iPod connection		■
Satellite navigation		na
6 CD changer		■
Metallic paint		**£360**

Options in **bold** fitted to test car
■ = Standard na = not available

EQUIPMENT CHECKLIST

17-inch alloy wheels	■
Automatic climate control	■
Xenon headlights	■
Trip computer	■
Leather/alcantara seats	■
Cruise control	■
Hands-free phone kit	**£135**
Front/side/curtain airbags	■
Keyless entry	■

RANGE AT A GLANCE

ENGINES

1.5 R	106bhp	£12,495
2.0 R	148bhp	£14,995
2.0 RX	148bhp	£17,495
2.5 WRX	227bhp	£19,995
2.5 WRX STi	296bhp	£24,995

TRANSMISSIONS

6-speed manual	std
4-speed auto	
(not WRX or STi)	£1,000

LEFT STi gets more aluminium-effect plastic around centre console, on steering wheel boss and around door pulls; better-quality interior is still below average, but offers good oddment storage; leather and Alcantara seats provide reasonable comfort for rear passengers.

SPECIFICATIONS IMPREZA STi

DIMENSIONS

Front track 1,530mm **Rear track** 1,540mm **Width including mirrors** 1,795mm

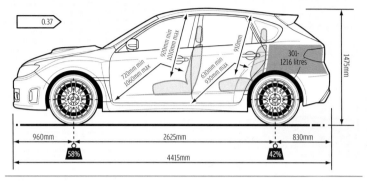

ENGINE

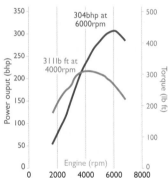

304bhp at 6000rpm

311lb ft at 4000rpm

Power ouput (bhp)

Torque (lb ft)

Engine (rpm)

Installation	Front, longitudinal
Type	4 cyls, horizontally opposed, 2,457cc, petrol, turbo
Made of	Alloy head and block
Bore/stroke	99.5/79.0mm
Compression ratio	8.2:1
Valve gear	4 per cyl
Power	296bhp at 6,000rpm
Torque	300lb ft at 4,000rpm
Red line	6,700rpm
Power to weight	197bhp per tonne
Torque to weight	199lb ft per tonne
Specific output	120bhp per litre

TRANSMISSION

Gearbox 6-speed manual

Ratios/mph per 1,000rpm

Final drive ratio 3.900

1st 3.64/5.2		2nd 2.24/8.5	
3rd 1.59/12.0		4th 1.14/16.7	
5th 0.89/21.4		6th 0.71/26.9	

CHASSIS AND BODY

Construction	Steel monocoque
Weight/as tested	1,505kg/1,530kg
Drag coefficient	0.36
Wheels	17in, alloy
Tyres	235/45 R17 (f), 235/45 R17 (r) Dunlop SP Sport 01
Spare	Space Saver

STEERING

Type Electrically assisted rack and pinion

Turns lock-to-lock 2.8

Turning circle 11.0m

SUSPENSION

Front MacPherson struts, coil springs, anti-roll bar

Rear Multi-link, coil springs, anti-roll bar

BRAKES

Front 330mm ventilated discs

Rear 305mm ventilated discs

Anti-lock Standard, EBD

RIDE AND HANDLING ★★★☆

Given the Impreza's demeanour and heritage, you'd expect the latest version to dart like a hare. Instead, it runs wide in corners that you merely steer through rather than charge, needing more lock than you'd expect. It's not understeer so much as slow turn-in, but it's a surprise.

Commit more speed to a bend and apply the throttle more forcibly and the Impreza suddenly appears to dig itself a set of grooves, displaying an urgent ambition to neutralise the faintest trace of understeer. This counter-intuitive reaction takes familiarisation but makes you aware of the Subaru's phenomenal cornering potential.

Lifting off produces little alteration of course, although a swift and decisive direction change had our car applying the ESP with thumping brutality on one occasion.

This near-instant change of personality makes the STi an unusual back-roads companion; it feels slightly unwilling if you're proceeding at an ambling-to-brisk pace, but almost manic with enthusiasm if you're feeling the same way. It's an enthusiasm that can be played with by altering the differential settings.

Auto minus is usually best, this setting working the rear axle harder to help turn in, the STi changing direction with more of the zeal you'd expect and, indeed, more of the enthusiasm than the previous STi mustered in the standard auto setting.

That is a clue to Subaru's philosophy. In its quest to broaden the Impreza's appeal and make it seem less extreme, it has made the car's default character blander to attract a broader trawl of drivers. Still, one benefit is a more pliant ride, this STi cresting sharp bumps at low speeds more calmly, although the promise of this improved suppleness isn't fully realised at high speeds, when you might expect a more loping gait.

No drivers will object to the excellence of the Brembo brakes or the improved, if still unexceptional, gearshift, but the quieter engine reveals too much road roar and general commotion of motion.

BUYING AND OWNING ★★★

This will not be a cheap car to buy, insure and fuel (at 18.1mpg), or pay any CO_2-based emissions taxes on, what with its 243g/km output. But it's good value for a powerful all-wheel-drive car; Subarus are

legendarily robust and hold their value reasonably well. The dealer network has a good reputation too, but you may have to travel a distance to find one, while repair costs can be high. And inner London use with this car is going to be prohibitive, the STi attracting the full £25 congestion charge rate for broaching the 225g/km threshold.

OPPOSITE "Oversized" rear spoiler; lamp clusters stuffed with LEDs.

ABOVE Blistered wheel arches, fatter wheels and bonnet air intake for STi.

AUTOCAR VERDICT

The STi is fast, grippy, robust, looks strange, has trick features, makes odd sounds and offers amazing value for money; it must be an Impreza. But this is a different kind of STi. Subaru's attempts to broaden the appeal of this car have given it a slightly odd, compromised character.

On the positive side, it is smoother, quieter, better finished, roomier, safer and more practical than its predecessor. But it's unlikely to tempt many premium car owners out of their seats, or even hot hatch buyers; the interior is still too cheap, the ride is too jostling and it's insufficiently refined for motorways. Meanwhile, hardcore enthusiasts will be disappointed by a dynamic personality that is almost bipolar, the shift between its languid mid-speed pace and its press-on dynamism too great to make it a thrilling car for enough of the time.

Split personality insufficient to outpoint the best hot hatches ★★★★✫